THE AMERICAN STUDENT'S
FREEDOM OF EXPRESSION

There is a limit to the legitimate interference of collective opinion with individual independence; and to find that limit, and maintain it against encroachment, is as indispensable to a good condition of human affairs, as protection against political despotism.

But though this proposition is not likely to be contested in general terms, the practical question, where to place the limit—how to make the fitting adjustment between individual independence and social control—is a subject on which nearly everything remains to be done. All that makes existence valuable to anyone, depends on the enforcement of restraints upon the actions of other people. Some rules of conduct, therefore, must be imposed, by law in the first place, and by opinion on many things which are not fit subjects for the operation of law. What these rules should be is the principal question in human affairs . . .

—John Stuart Mill, *On Liberty*

THE AMERICAN STUDENT'S FREEDOM OF EXPRESSION

A Research Appraisal

by E. G. WILLIAMSON and JOHN L. COWAN

WITH THE EDITORIAL COLLABORATION OF R. GEORGE CRAWFORD
AND VIRGINIA WILLEMS

The University of Minnesota Press, Minneapolis

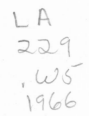

Preface

FOLLOWING the Supreme Court's 1954 desegregation decision it became evident that vast cultural shifts were in the making. A few college students began to seek solutions to divisive social issues, to experiment with passive methods of social transformation, and to examine and criticize radical alternatives. The growth of student organization for social action prompted educators to reconsider fundamental educational assumptions. What are the purposes of higher education? Do colleges and universities deliberately restrain students from active participation in society's problems? And, if so, is this a responsible position? To what extent, if any, should institutions oppose or support political views? Are constitutional rights of students actually infringed, either intentionally or unknowingly, by college administrators and faculty? Should some consideration be given to a binding statement of student academic freedom? These are only a few of the questions that needed answers.

In the spring of 1961 the president of the National Association of Student Personnel Administrators, uneasy about conventional administrative response and sensitive to the inflammatory possibilities of emerging campus conflict, appointed members to a study commission. The committee of eleven deans was asked to examine and appraise the responsibilities of student personnel administrators in connection with student discussion of social issues. This required analysis of educational goals and objectives and called for answers which rested on foundations of cherished and deeply ingrained values. But, as do all questions of

214-94

value, these also involved many questions of fact. Thus, the members of the study commission engaged in difficult tasks of appraisal involving complex and subtle relationships between facts and values—between what *is* and what *ought to be*.

The purpose of the commission was, in part, to initiate a definition of student academic freedom. The members first reviewed published material about student rights, and they rapidly arrived at one conclusion earlier stated by Professor Sydney Hook: "There is more sloppy rhetoric per page about academic freedom by those who believe that they are supporting, and those intent on criticizing it, than on any other theme with the possible exception of democracy." To be sure, there were educational treatises, but these were not generally addressed to institutional relationships with students. And there were important formal declarations of desired student rights. The United States National Student Association had published a statement as early as 1947, and a similar statement by the American Civil Liberties Union was circulating. Moreover, the American Association of University Professors was about to formulate a statement of principles underlying faculty responsibility for student academic freedom. Several writers had recently examined, or were in the process of analyzing, the constitutional basis of the students' claim to rights in the academic community. But no comprehensive research studies reporting facts about student freedom or institutional restraints on student expression were to be found.

Commission members reasoned that a setting forth of relevant facts was necessary if universities were to practice the academic inquiry to which they subscribed in theory. Yet the deans on the commission realized that facts alone would not answer their questions, nor could all relevant data be collected in a single study. They hoped by their work to obtain answers to some of the major questions about academic freedom for students, and also to stimulate other researchers.

Therefore, the study presented in the following pages is almost solely addressed to the question of what *is* rather than what *ought to be*. The authors—Williamson, the director of the study, and Cowan, the technical director—have selected material from literally millions of data "bits"; they have necessarily interpreted, summarized, generalized, simplified, asked questions, and suggested possible explanatory hypotheses for the results. Thus, their own value assumptions have influenced the presentation but these are evident enough for the discerning reader to identify them and make allowances in arriving at his own interpretation of the data. The writers have planned together, examined and analyzed data together; they have written chapters together and criticized and edited the manuscript to the point where it is not possible, even if it were desirable, to assert which author wrote what words. They have attempted to stay close to the data and accordingly the style of the report is frequently statistical. The matter of style is noted without apology, however, because the language of fact is that which has been so noticeably absent in recent controversies about student rights.

The organization of the study is simple and straightforward. Brief examination of the table of contents shows the pattern of presentation. Still, three research methods deserve special mention. First, the nature of student freedom of expression in American colleges is assessed by comparing and contrasting the perceptions of five different groups of respondents: presidents, deans of students, chairmen of faculty committees on student affairs, student body presidents, and student newspaper editors. This is not a one-sided report by deans of students even though their national professional organization sponsored the study. Second, data are presented by geographical region—in terms of the boundaries of regional accrediting associations. This was done with the intent of making data accessible to, and meaningful for, educational planners as they work in existing associations. Third, data are reported in terms of ten categories of higher educational institutions: large and small public universities, technical institutions, teachers' colleges, private (nonsectarian) universities and liberal arts colleges, Protestant universities and liberal arts colleges, and Catholic universities and liberal arts colleges. Thus, the relative freedom of these schools is clear.

Recognizing that readers vary in their interest and motivation the authors suggest four alternative paths to be followed for the most profitable examination of the book. Busy persons familiar with discussions about student freedom who want a rapid, non-statistical summary should read Chapter 8, "Where Is Freedom Enjoyed?" Readers wanting some background on current issues as well as a summary of the findings should read Chapter 1, "Rationale and Research Design," and Chapter 8. For a thorough reading by persons unfamiliar with statistics, Chapter 1 should be emphasized and the remainder of the book should be read. Persons engaged in or planning similar research should read the entire book. (Write to the authors c/o Office of the Dean of Students,

University of Minnesota, for copies of the questionnaires and mimeographed copies of statistical supplements.)

In order to achieve a high rate of questionnaire return for this study it was necessary to assure each respondent that his reply would not be identified either by name or by institution and that such information would be known only to the research staff. For this reason the degrees of freedom of student expression in specific colleges and universities have not been compared and the relative standings of identified institutions have not been presented. Moreover, in order to hold to this pledge of confidentiality it is not possible to release identified data to other investigators. From a research standpoint this is regrettable, but because of the highly flammable controversies that had arisen and the political implications of many of the responses the precaution was imperative.

Finally, the authors emphasize that the results reported in this study should not be considered fixed and immutable. The cultural context in which our colleges and universities seek to fulfill their mission is fluid and dynamic. Issues are resolved and new and often more complex problems emerge. The ebb and flow of national and international political tides will affect the freedoms which students exercise. The data presented here represent only one point on a time-sequence curve. Nonetheless, the authors hope that these data contribute a broad and realistic perspective to administrators, professors, and students preparing to initiate or currently engaged in discussions about college policies governing student affairs. Higher educational institutions must continually—and especially at the present time—reassess relationships with students, redefine or make explicit their educational goals and objectives, and seek to secure the degree and types of freedom necessary for students responsibly to achieve high-quality education. It is to be hoped, too, that other researchers will be encouraged, now and in the future, to search into the thickets of academic organization and student life to find answers to the perplexing problems of academic administration and to locate other points on the curve, for only with additional studies and experiments executed with better designs and greater precision will the secrets be revealed.

E. G. WILLIAMSON
JOHN L. COWAN

University of Minnesota

Acknowledgments

A COMPREHENSIVE research effort such as the present study is conceived and brought to fruition by many persons. We gratefully acknowledge all who had a part in the study—the originators, the conceptualizers, the underwriters, the consultants, the participants, and the implementers.

The idea for the study was suggested by Deans Glen Nygreen, Donald Winbigler, and O. D. Roberts within the Executive Committee of the National Association of Student Personnel Administrators during the presidency of William S. Guthrie (1960–1961). The members of the Executive Committee (listed on p. xiii) unanimously approved the proposal and authorized the president to appoint an *ad hoc* study commission. William Guthrie gave a rationale for the work of the commission in his presidential address to the association on April 3, 1961 ("Three Hats for the Deans—and Three Cheers," published in the *Proceedings* of the association).

The members of the study commission narrowed the idea into researchable proportions. It is in notes from their meetings and in their correspondence files that one finds many questions asked, many viewpoints expressed, many positions considered, and many plans ruled out. Finally, a proposal for research was drafted and formalized. The commission members working on these problems and others at later stages cannot be given enough credit. In addition to drafting the proposal, these persons evaluated and criticized proposed questionnaires, urged their colleagues to participate in the study, wrote follow-up letters, and read and examined voluminous preliminary reports. These jobs were performed so tirelessly that we have listed each member on a following page; to each goes our sincere appreciation.

Long before some of the implications of contemporary student desires were made vividly clear to the public by the actions of the Free Speech Movement at the University of California, Berkeley, foundations were asked to underwrite our research proposal. The study was delayed more than one year because many of the larger private foundations were unwilling to fund research of such a "controversial" nature. Presumably, to these foundations, the relevance of the study to contemporary problems of higher education was not obvious in 1962. The Edward W. Hazen Foundation, with a historic concern for student values and student welfare, was predisposed to evaluate the proposal more carefully. We extend our thanks to the Hazen board of directors, their able chairman, President John Nason of Carleton College, and their farsighted president, Dr. Paul J. Braisted. They have been a constant source of encouragement and financial support.

We deeply appreciate the willingness of our University of Minnesota consultants to bring their professional expertise to bear upon our sampling problems, details of questionnaire construction, mailing procedures, and analysis techniques: Dr. Raymond O. Collier, Dr. John Neter, Dr. David P. Campbell, Dr. Elaine Walster, and Dr. David J. Weiss. We especially esteem the contributions of a friend and colleague who did not live to see the completion of the study—Dr. Ben Willerman, who, at the time of the study, was on leave from the University of Minnesota working as staff associate for the Social Science Research Council. Dr. Marvin Stein, director of the Numerical Analysis Center of the University of Minnesota, made available computer facilities and consultants.

Almost four thousand persons thoughtfully responded to our questionnaires. By agreement with them, they shall remain anonymous, but the educational institutions which they represented are listed in the Appendix. We especially thank our many "research agents"—the deans of students, who served to interpret and coordinate the study on their campuses; the presidents, who took time from pressing administrative duties; and the students, who took a constructively critical look at their freedom. Their perceptions of student freedom were indispensable.

Finally, we come to the relatively small group of persons who implemented the study proposal. We were very fortunate that Sharon M. Nelson possessed the skill of computer programming and was willing to use it for our benefit. Many research assistants helped us sort, winnow, and evaluate computer output for reports: we especially acknowledge the assistance of James Tintner, Ravina Gelfand, and Charles Ehrensperger. Manuscript typing and clerical assistance were provided by Anita Norman, Jeanlee Hovious, Judith Strohl, Lynne Nichols, and Joyce Mayberg. La Donna Becker, Virginia Drake, and Dean Carl Knox, University of Illinois, secretary-treasurer of NASPA, assisted with budgeting and accounting. R. George Crawford and Virginia Willems collaborated with us in the writing of the final manuscript, and for their insight and skill we have deep admiration. There are others, too, and while we cannot mention all by name, we acknowledge their contributions.

Many persons contributed to and brought this report into being. Where it is rational, they sharpened our reason. Where it is penetrating, they gave us insight. Yet, finally, we are responsible for evaluating, shaping, interpreting, and presenting the data. If it lacks generality, we did not see the forest for the trees. If it lacks force, we did not energize it. And if there are errors (we hope we eliminated them), we are at fault. Even the computers will not accept responsibility: someone had to tell them what to do!

E. G. W.

J. L. C.

Members of the
Study Commission on "The Student and Social Issues"

E. G. Williamson, Dean of Students, University of Minnesota, Chairman and Director of the Study

Donald K. Anderson, Dean of Students, University of Washington

Homer D. Babbidge, Jr., President, University of Connecticut

Armour J. Blackburn, Dean of Students, Howard University

Willard W. Blaesser, Dean of Students, City College of the City University of New York

Hugh Borton, President, Haverford College

Thomas J. Edwards, Dean of Students, Kenyon College

James R. Kreuzer, Acting Dean of Students, Queens College of the City University of New York

O. W. Lacy, Dean of Students, Trinity College (Connecticut)

Daniel H. Pollitt, Professor, Law School, University of North Carolina

Reverend Patrick H. Ratterman, S.J., Dean of Men, Xavier University

Walter B. Rea, Dean of Students, University of Michigan

David W. Robinson, Dean of Student Affairs, Emory University

W. Dennis Shaul, Student, Law School, Harvard University

Donald Stewart, Student, Law School, University of Alabama

W. L. Swartzbaugh, Associate Dean of the College, Amherst College

Helen White, Professor, English Department, University of Wisconsin

Contents

LIST OF TABLES

LIST OF FIGURES

THE AMERICAN STUDENT'S
FREEDOM OF EXPRESSION

1 ⁄

Rationale and Research Design

DISCUSSIONS of student academic freedom have seldom been academic. Indeed the atmosphere in which they have proceeded has usually been highly charged with sharp accusations and impassioned pleas for action. In contrast, this present study is an attempt to apply one of the basic tools of scholarship—research—to the problems of student freedom which beset the academic world. Before turning to the more limited task of describing how much and what types of freedom exist and where, we will first briefly delineate the two sides of the basic issue. Although we do not attempt to resolve the current conflict, we do provide the antagonists with a factual account of the present situation and thus hope to contribute to a rational resolution.

Those who maintain that academic freedom for college students must be severely limited have two main lines of argument. The first emphasizes the inappropriateness of granting freedom to students. Because of their traditionally and officially subordinate status, students should be seen and not heard. They should not intervene with words or action in issues which divide our society, since such serious matters are best left to older and wiser heads. The second argument stresses the dangers of granting freedom to the intellectually and emotionally immature. Proponents of this view say that students, because of their youth and lack of training, are likely to reach the wrong conclusions if left to grapple with academic problems singlehandedly. Some have added that students not only make serious errors in judgment but also, because of their emotional immaturity, sometimes deliberately abuse liberties. Unless they are kept under careful surveillance their penchant for uncontrolled outbursts might seriously disrupt the educational processes of the college, offending its patrons and endangering its prosperity and continued existence. These arguments are based on a conception of the college as a place where the young must be taught the "truth" as it is known by older men, and where living and thinking habits must be strictly supervised while truth is revealed.

Those who maintain that academic freedom for college students is desirable recognize its value as a pedagogical tool. The proponents of this view would maintain that it is healthy for students to address themselves to society's problems while in college, since this provides training for the responsibilities they will assume, or may have already assumed, as voting citizens. In answer to the argument that students will misuse liberty, they would argue that the right to use one's freedoms unwisely must be protected as firmly as the right to use them wisely, and that only through the use of freedom, and sometimes its abuse, can its responsible exercise be learned. These men would argue that freedom cannot be taught in a vacuum or dangled as a reward. Those who offer such arguments frequently share Milton's faith in the strength of truth expressed in the *Areopagitica*: "And though all the winds of doctrine were let loose to play upon the earth, so Truth be in the field, we do injuriously by licensing and prohibiting to misdoubt her strength. Let her and Falsehood grapple; who ever knew Truth put to the worse, in a free and open encounter. Her confuting is the best and surest suppressing."

Historical Development of Student Freedom

Early American colleges were modeled on the British residential university in which teaching rather than research was emphasized. At Harvard, the country's oldest college, founded in 1636, little freedom was accorded its students either in their choice of curriculum, which heavily emphasized the classics, or in their way of life. This pattern was typical of other early American colleges. For example, the charter of the University of Pennsylvania specifically directed the college administrators to regulate manners, morals, and dress of the students; and at the

4

University of Georgia strict rules were adopted and enforced to control every aspect of student behavior, even habits of speech. Thus was established a tradition of regimentation in which the college acted in place of the parent as the molder of character for what were then considered to be morally perverse and intellectually innocent students.

In loco parentis continued to be the guiding principle of American higher education well into the nineteenth century and may persist in some institutions today. As late as 1913, Berea College in Kentucky passed a rule prohibiting its students from patronizing any off-campus restaurants. One restaurant, dependent entirely on student patronage, took its complaint to court, but the court upheld the college ruling:

College authorities stand *in loco parentis* concerning the physical and moral welfare and mental training of pupils. For the purposes of this case, the school, its officers and students are a legal entity, as much so as any family, and, like a father may direct his children, those in charge of boarding schools are well within their rights and powers when they direct their students what to eat and where they may get it; where they may go and what forms of amusement are forbidden.[1]

The colonial college became the modern university largely through following the German model. In the late eighteenth and early nineteenth centuries a new type of institution was established in Germany—the research university—and with it originated a concept of academic freedom. This freedom was twofold in scope, guaranteeing both *Lehrfreiheit* and *Lernfreiheit*. *Lehrfreiheit* was the professor's freedom to conduct inquiry on any topic and to "profess" the conclusions of his research. He was free within the classroom to teach the students what he felt to be the truth, and he could advance his views by whatever methods he chose. However, he was expected to avoid subjects of current political controversy as being too immediate to permit dispassionate analysis, and outside of the classroom he was expected to support all government policies as a loyal civil servant. At the same time that the professor commanded so much authority over subject and method in the classroom, the student was free to accept or reject the professor and his views as well as to determine his own way of life. This was the essence of *Lernfreiheit*, which permitted the student to transfer among universities at will, exempted him from compulsory class attendance, let him choose his own curriculum, held him responsible for only one

---

[1] Gott v. Berea College, 156 Ky. 376, 161 S.W. 204 (1913).

state-administered comprehensive examination at the end of his studies, and allowed him to live where and how he chose. Within this framework of freedom many students dissipated their college years in riotous living, while others became the disciples of certain professors and attained great scholarly distinction.

Academic freedom was so attractive to American scholars that they began leaving en masse to study in German universities. By 1890 this exodus consisted of more than 2,000 advanced scholars, and before the century was over more than 9,000 Americans had studied at German universities.[2] When these men returned to the United States, they brought with them the concept and ideal of *Lehrfreiheit,* and they fought to establish freedom for professors in this country.

Three circumstances conditioned the form of *Lehrfreiheit* as it was introduced to America. First, America was a democracy, and so the professor was free outside the classroom to advocate whatever political position he chose. Second, a lay board of control governed the American college, unlike its British or German counterpart, and this limited the faculty's freedom in determining institutional policies, while at the same time it provided a buffer between the faculty and the pressure of the government, which protected the American professor's political freedom. Third, the American land-grant college was designed to meet the immediate, practical needs of society: to provide "know-how" for American industry and agriculture, not dispassionate analysis of abstract or historical problems. These factors led to relatively less freedom within the classroom, where the American professor was expected to teach the facts and methods of a discipline rather than his own views on life, and to relatively greater freedom outside the classroom.

While the practices of *Lehrfreiheit* were adapted to American needs, *Lernfreiheit,* or students' freedom, was not imported at all. There was, for one thing, the long tradition of regimentation in American colleges. Also, undergraduate students did not migrate to Germany; they were undoubtedly largely unaware that students elsewhere in the world enjoyed considerable liberty. And American professors, struggling for their own freedom, were perhaps too hard pressed to champion the

[2] Charles Franklin Thwing, *The American and the German University, One Hundred Years of History* (New York, 1928), pp. 41–42, as cited by Richard Hofstadter and Walter P. Metzger, *The Development of Academic Freedom in the United States* (New York: Columbia University Press, 1955), pp. 367–368.

students' cause or to give it much attention. When the American Association of University Professors issued a report on academic freedom in 1915, they made no mention of students' freedom. While the struggle for professors' freedom raged, students remained quiet.

The Environment of Current Conflict

In general, the professors have won their freedom although it was challenged as recently as the McCarthy era. Today students are fighting to win theirs. To be sure, in 1907 Charles W. Eliot delivered an address on "Academic Freedom" to Harvard's Phi Beta Kappa chapter in which he discussed the student's freedom to choose his studies, to refuse to attend chapel, to compete on even terms for scholarships, and to select his own friends. At that time the consideration of student liberties was uncommon, but today everyone has joined in the debate. The National Student Association, the American Civil Liberties Union, and the American Association of University Professors have issued statements outlining what they feel to be desirable freedoms for students. In some cases the issues have been taken to court so that the judiciary has begun to establish guidelines in this area.

What do the students want?

In 1947 the National Student Association, whose membership consists of student government officers throughout the United States, specified the "rights" which it contended American students should enjoy. First this group listed the right of the individual to college admission without discrimination. Once admitted, individual students should also have the right to expect clear, precise written regulations and procedural due process in disciplinary actions, as well as the right to travel, to exercise citizenship rights, and to avoid double jeopardy (a much misunderstood issue). Student organizations should have the right to have official recognition, to use campus facilities, to choose a faculty adviser, to invite speakers, and to refuse to disclose membership lists. There is the right to establish and issue student-managed publications. Student government should have the right to enjoy democratic processes, to set activitity fees, to determine the codes of student conduct, and to participate in institutional policy-making. These statements generally represent what students desire today.

In succeeding decades, a few such suits were heard, with decisions generally in favor of the institution. In the Syracuse case,[3] for example, the court upheld the power of the institution to require a student, before admission, to sign a statement that she agreed to abide by every established or potential regulation. Today such extensive power would not be sanctioned.

In a series of decisions terminating in the Dixon case[4] two principles of law have emerged as criteria for the legality of an institution's rules. The first is that the rule must be necessary to the accomplishment of the mission of the institution as defined in the charter, and the second is that the exercise of authority must be reasonable. Thus, an institution cannot exceed the powers granted by or implied in its charter, and it may well be refused even these powers if the courts find their exercise to be "unreasonable." Although the courts, since their definition of *in loco parentis,* have not decisively redefined the relationship between the public university and its students, judicial interest in matters arising out of this relationship has intensified and the inclination seems to be increasingly toward upholding student freedoms.

Some students, however, do not seem willing to wait for the slow judicial process to define their freedoms. For example, during the academic year 1964–65, after this study's data had been collected, riotous demonstrations took place on the Berkeley campus of the University of California. The leaders of these disturbances called their organization the "Free Speech Movement." The demonstrations were precipitated by the university's sudden enforcement of a long-neglected policy: students were forbidden to engage in political solicitation on property adjacent to the university, property which many of them believed did not belong to the university. Although these students enjoyed a relatively high degree of freedom in their university, they found restrictions that remained (primarily concerning political activities) intolerable. Whether or not it was aptly named in this instance, the Free Speech Movement enlisted wide and serious support—sometimes vociferously expressed—on many other campuses across the country.

[3] Anthony v. Syracuse University, 130 Misc. 249, 223 N.Y. Supp. 796 (Sup. Ct. 1927).
[4] Dixon v. Alabama State Board of Education, 294 F. 2d 150 (CA 5 1961) Cert. denied 368 U.S. 930 (1961).

8

Objectives of the Study

"Freedom" is a broad term. It can mean anything from voluntary chapel attendance to a state of anarchy. The freedom with which our present study is concerned is student academic freedom rather narrowly defined. Three types of student freedom can be distinguished: freedom within the curriculum, social freedom for the individual, and freedom for students to organize themselves in various ways to express their views. It is the latter which we designate as student academic freedom in this study.

Freedom within the curriculum involves such issues as elective courses, compulsory class attendance, grading systems, and examination procedures. These are not matters of current controversy except as relatively isolated local issues. It also involves the quality of instruction, methods of teaching, and the size of classes. Although these problems are quite properly of vital interest to both professors and students, they have assumed secondary importance in the current debate.

Social freedom for individuals involves residence hall or fraternity rules, standards of conduct, and disciplinary procedures. The liberty to live off campus, to have a car, or to transgress the community's moral code or standards of good taste may also be at issue. The chief concern of students here is that just, explicit rules be established to provide safeguards against arbitrary or inequitable administration. Like freedom within the curriculum, this issue has existed as long as the institution of higher learning itself.

Academic freedom, as it is defined in this present study, is a more recent issue but now one of the most urgent concerns of students. It is the freedom to organize new student groups or to utilize established student groups to express views more or less actively concerned with the issues which divide our society. Many educators maintain that political interests of college students today are markedly different from those of a generation past. While many students formerly interested themselves in broad social issues only to make sport of the few "excessively earnest" crusaders, students now take issues such as nuclear weapons, the Vietnam conflict, and the civil rights struggle very seriously indeed, and have become crusaders themselves. When students form organizations to express views on these controversial issues, they are likely to step on some of society's more sensitive toes, and the pain is transmitted through the medium of angry letters to the nerve center

9

of the college administration. Since the college is dependent on the parents who have sent their children to it and on other outside sources for financial support, and since college administrators sometimes themselves believe student actions to be ill-advised, the administration occasionally acts to curtail the activities of these student groups. This is the issue on which the battle lines are currently drawn (thirteen of the sixteen National Student Association "rights" bear on this point), and it is also the central concern of our study.

How much freedom of this kind do students enjoy now, and which colleges have granted the most freedom, or the least? How much more freedom do students want and what types of colleges are under the most pressure? What forces prevent the expansion of freedom and how effective are they? What are the optimum amount and the forms of freedom that best fulfill the objectives of education and how can they be enacted? This last question is the crux of the present debate. But before it can be answered we must determine how much academic freedom (as defined above) students enjoy now and which colleges have granted the most freedom or the least. In answering this question we hope also to identify some of the difficulties in enacting desirable forms of freedom.

Assumptions of the Study

Within the area of academic freedom for student organizations there is a wide range of issues. On the basis of both the published statements of the National Student Association, the American Association of University Professors, and the American Civil Liberties Union, and the experiences of members of Commission VIII of the National Association of Student Personnel Administrators, reported to us in research planning meetings, we have assumed that certain specific issues are of the greatest concern to students. These were the issues we investigated. They are four in number.

Free speech is a venerable American freedom, yet many college students claim they do not enjoy it. They contend that their organizations and newspapers are unable to express certain viewpoints, or sometimes any viewpoint at all, on issues of the most vital importance to American society. We sought to determine the basis for this complaint.

Students assert that their interest in society's problems leads them to invite speakers who are actively working to resolve problems of national moment, and that college administrations interfere with their right to issue these invitations. We gathered data which indicate whether and where this is true.

After hearing about society's problems, students want to solve them. They want to petition their congressman, picket the White House, or pass a strongly worded referendum. They say that their colleges often will not permit these activities. We also gathered data on this point.

When we were devising our questionnaires civil rights seemed to be the most controversial issue of the time. We assumed that because college policies would have been recently tested in this area differences among them would be especially detectable. Therefore, many of our questions bore on this subject.

In addition to selecting these four issues within which to investigate the extent of academic freedom for student organizations, we assumed that the structure of any particular institution is related to the extent of freedom practiced there and to the ease with which existing freedoms can be expanded. We therefore gathered data on three aspects of institutional structure.

The student newspaper editor is perhaps the most widely read representative of the student body. His editorial page and the news he finds worthy of publication not only reflect but also shape the views and interests of the students. His independence is thus of considerable interest as it provides him freedom both to express certain views and to lead students in demanding more rights. In seeking to determine the degree of the student editor's independence we gathered information concerning his sources of financial support and the subtle or overt ways in which censorship could be exercised over student publications.

The student body president is another important student leader whose independence may reflect both the extent of student freedom and the availability of leadership for new student movements to gain more freedom. We gathered information concerning his functions and sources of financial support.

Finally, the administration may sometimes form its policies without really knowing what the students want or how students will react. This practice probably results in emotionalized resentment on both sides and thus may delay the adoption of rational, thoughtfully examined policies. Therefore, we gathered data regarding the extent of student

11

participation on policy-making committees and the perceived usefulness of students as members of these committees.

Since all these are matters of current debate, and since students and administrators seemed to disagree concerning the extent of freedom which actually exists on the campus, we did not assume that any one person on a campus could accurately reflect a generally perceived degree of student freedom. Thus, a student might say that students would not be permitted to picket a public meeting and an administrator might say that they could. In order to determine whether administrators and students perceived the situations on their campuses in the same way, we asked many of the same questions of both students and administrators. This was our attempt to determine whether incongruity of perception was a source of confusion and conflict.

Procedure of the Study

According to our research design five individuals were to be questioned in each college or university included in the population of four-year American higher educational institutions. These five individuals were the president and the dean of students as administrators, the student body president and student newspaper editor as student leaders, and the chairman of the faculty committee on student affairs.

We assumed that each of these people could respond in three capacities. Each was a perceiver of the status quo: he could tell us how much freedom he perceived on his campus with respect to the specific issues we designated. He was a leader who could speak with authority about the forces which influenced him in making decisions and the principles which he personally tried to apply. He was also in a position to assess the strength of the forces at work to expand or restrict the extent of student freedom, and to judge whether these forces were increasing or diminishing.

The *Directory of Higher Education, 1961–1962* was used to select the population of colleges and universities to be invited to participate in the study. The population was composed of 1,000 regionally-accredited, four-year, baccalaureate-degree-granting institutions with enrollment of more than 100 students. All federally controlled institutions (primarily the military academies) were excluded except for Howard University, which is only partly supported by federal funds. Seminaries, art schools, and proprietary colleges were also excluded. Independent

12

campuses of large universities were considered as separate institutions (see Appendix).

In order to secure the participation of as many of the 1,000 institutions as possible, the 1963–64 president of the National Association of Student Personnel Administrators, Dean James C. McLeod, Northwestern University, wrote to the person functioning as dean of students (by whatever title) in each college to ask him to act as our research representative on his campus. Each dean was asked to introduce the purposes and procedures for the study to other designated respondents and to inform us of his institution's willingness to participate in the study. We waged an intensive campaign of letters, telephone calls, and telegrams to those deans who were hesitant to serve as our research representative. As a result more than 800 had agreed to cooperate by the time questionnaires were mailed to them (April 1964).

Questionnaires were distributed by the following methods: The president of each college which had not specifically declined to participate received his questionnaire with a personal letter. The letter stated the purpose of the study and solicited the president's personal attention to his questionnaire. This letter also named the person we had asked to serve as research agent and indicated either that he had agreed or that we had received no reply from him. Questionnaires for each respondent, except the president, were mailed to those deans who had replied and indicated their willingness to assist us. At that time they were asked to complete and return their questionnaire and to distribute the others to the appropriate persons. If their schools did not have persons functioning as either student newspaper editor, student body president, or chairman of a faculty committee on student affairs, the deans were requested to inform us of that fact by returning the blank questionnaire with explanatory notations.

Respondents were asked to complete their own pre-stamped questionnaires and return them *directly* to our research office. To ensure a high level of response we also assured all respondents that their replies would be confidential and that no individual or institutional response would be identified in our reports.

Response to the Study

At the crucial stage of the study when questionnaires were being returned, we relied heavily on the very helpful support from the deans of students. Where necessary we sought their follow-up assistance. The result of these intensive efforts was excellent. By August 10, 1964, when we began our analysis, 85 per cent of the colleges had returned one or more of the five questionnaires and almost 70 per cent had returned all five. Table 1 presents the final results in more detail.

Table 1. Institutional Participation in the Study[a]

Response to Invitation	No. of Institutions
None	26
Declined to participate	87
Accepted but did not return questionnaires	38
Accepted and returned one or more questionnaires	849
All five returned	695
Four returned	90
Three returned	34
Two returned	10
One returned	20

[a] Despite repeated efforts to persuade all the institutions in the population to respond to an invitation to participate in the study, no reply of any kind was received from 26 colleges. Only presidents' questionnaires accompanied by final appeals to participate were sent to these 26 institutions. Questionnaires were not mailed to the 87 institutions declining participation. Only the 887 institutions accepting our invitation to participate received all questionnaires. Ninety-six per cent (849) of these 887 institutions returned one or more questionnaires, and 78 per cent (695) returned all five questionnaires.

We received usable questionnaires from 757 presidents, 813 deans of students, 807 student body presidents, and 785 student newspaper editors. Of the 800 returned faculty chairman questionnaires only 55 per cent were completed by persons identifying themselves as faculty chairmen per se; 26 per cent were completed by deans of students who also served as chairmen of the faculty policy-making committees at their institutions, and 19 per cent were returned blank with the explanation that there was no faculty committee for making policy concerning student affairs. Of the group of 695 schools which returned all five questionnaires, nine schools indicated, by returning blank questionnaires with notes, that they had no student newspaper, three had no president at the time of the study, three had no dean of students, and 123 had no faculty committee on student affairs.

Characteristics of Respondents

There is great diversity among the 1,000 colleges which constitute our population, and it was necessary to determine whether the institutions from which we received responses were representative of all of them. Some colleges enroll men, some women, and others both. Some have a large private endowment, others are publicly supported. Enrollments at these colleges ranged from 100 to 35,000 students, and at any one institution there might be only white students, or only Negroes, or both. Some institutions are based on and inculcate religious ideals, others are devoted to the pragmatic concerns of agriculture, the arts, or the sciences. Some train teachers, others train researchers, and still others emphasize breadth of education. These colleges are scattered through all the regions of our country, and their students come from different locations, have a variety of backgrounds, and demonstrate widely diverging interests.

To determine whether we received questionnaires in the proper proportion from each type of institution, we devised six criteria by which all 1,000 colleges were classified. These variables of classification were sex of students, race of students, geographical region of the school's location, size of enrollment, curriculum offered, and type of control. Thus, regarding sex of students, the school would be classified as a men's college, a women's college, or a coeducational institution. The same school would also be classified according to whether it was controlled by the public, by a Protestant or a Roman Catholic group, or by a private board. The criteria by which each school was classified are listed below.

Variables of Classification

A. Sex of students
   1. Coeducational institutions
   2. Men's colleges
   3. Women's colleges
B. Racial characteristics of students
   1. Colleges with predominantly white enrollment
   2. Colleges with predominantly Negro enrollment

15

C. Geographical accrediting region
  1. New England
  2. Middle Atlantic
  3. North Central
  4. Northwestern
  5. Southern
  6. Western
D. Size of enrollment
  1. Fewer than 1,000 students
  2. 1,000–2,499 students
  3. 2,500–3,999 students
  4. 4,000–10,999 students
  5. 11,000 or more students
E. Curricular emphasis
  1. Universities—two or more colleges, offering of advanced degrees
  2. Liberal arts colleges
  3. Technical institutions
  4. State and/or teachers' colleges (emphasis on teacher education)
F. Type of control
  1. Public (state and municipal control)
  2. Private (nonsectarian)
  3. Protestant
  4. Roman Catholic

The 1,000 schools of the population were classified according to these six criteria and the number of schools in each category was recorded. The schools which returned all five questionnaires were also classified and compared with the corresponding proportion in the population as a whole, using the chi-square "Goodness of Fit" test. In terms of proportionate representation there are no significant differences between the population of 1,000 schools and the group of 695 schools which returned all five questionnaires with respect to sex, race, regional accreditation, size, curriculum, or type of institutional control. Figure 1 illustrates the distribution of both the population and the sample of 695 schools by these criteria.

The same procedure was followed to determine the representativeness of institutions which returned one or more questionnaires, the group of schools from which the president's questionnaire was returned, and the groups returning the dean's, faculty chairman's, student body presi-

PER CENT OF SCHOOLS

		0	10	20	30	40	50	60	70	80	90	100

Sex

		Coeducational		Men's	Women's
	Population	75%		9%	15%
	Sample	76%		9%	15%

Race

		White		Negro
	Population	94%		6%
	Sample	95%		5%

Geographical Accrediting Region

		New England	Middle Atlantic	North Central	North West	South	West
	Population	9%	21%	36%	6%	24%	5%
	Sample	8%	20%	41%	6%	20%	5%

Size of Enrollment

		999 or less	1000-2499	2500-3999	4000-10,999	11,000 or more
	Population	40%	31%	9%	14%	6%
	Sample	39%	32%	9%	14%	7%

Curriculum

		Universities	Liberal Arts Colleges	Technical	Teachers'
	Population	25%	51%	5%	20%
	Sample	26%	50%	4%	19%

Institutional Control

		Public	Private	Protestant	Catholic
	Population	34%	22%	24%	20%
	Sample	34%	22%	23%	21%

NOTE: The sample considered here is composed of the 695 institutions (69.5 % of the population of 1,000 schools) from which all five questionnaires were returned. Use of this sample in this report permits comparisons among the various respondent groups.

Percentages may not total to 100 due to rounding error.

Figure 1. Distribution of 695 Responding Institutions on Six Variables of Classification Compared to Distribution of Population of 1,000 Institutions

dent's, and student editor's questionnaires. It was found that each of these groups was representative of the entire population of schools with respect to all the categories listed. Thus, the conclusion was reached that no category of schools was significantly underrepresented or over-represented.

Rather than present all results in terms of the unwieldy six criteria and twenty-four categories, we classified the colleges into ten categories based on the variables of size, curricular emphasis, and type of control. This classification has the advantage of simplicity and also reflects the categories which are typically used in describing colleges and universities. When our sample was grouped in terms of these ten categories and compared with the distribution of the entire population in the study among the same categories, the responding schools again proved to be representative (see Table 2).

17

Table 2. Categorization of Colleges and Universities

Type of Institution	Number in Population	Number in Sample	Percentage of Population in Sample
Public			
Large universities	58	45	77.6
Small universities	88	63	71.6
Teachers' colleges	175	119	68.0
Technical institutions	50	29	58.0
Private			
Universities			
Nonsectarian	64	45	70.3
Protestant	29	22	75.9
Catholic	34	27	79.4
Liberal arts colleges			
Nonsectarian	130	91	70.0
Protestant	214	137	64.0
Catholic	158	117	74.0
Total group	1,000	695	69.5

The sample is also representative of the various geographical regions of the United States. In making a regional analysis we used the six regions into which the United States is divided for purposes of college accreditation. These boundaries are indicated in Figure 2.

Figure 2. Geographical Accrediting Regions

Characteristics of Non-Respondents

Which schools did not return our questionnaires? Of the 1,000 colleges invited to participate, 38 indicated that they intended to respond but failed to do so in spite of letters of inquiry. We assume that in these cases the questionnaires proved too long or the administration was distracted by other concerns. Another 26 schools never answered our initial letters of invitation at all, and 87 explicitly declined to participate. Of those who refused most pleaded lack of staff or time to fill out our questionnaires. Others indicated that their student activities were in the process of major reorganization, suggesting that answers made at that time might be misleading. Some doubted the usefulness of questionnaire studies or thought the questions irrelevant to the organization or philosophy of their institutions.

Schools which did not respond were analyzed in terms of the known variables of size, race, sex, location, type of control, and curricular emphasis. The schools which did not respond were as diverse as those that did but several types of institutions responded *slightly* less often than the others. These were the southern colleges, the Protestant liberal arts colleges, the small colleges, the women's colleges, and the technical schools and teachers' colleges.

In an effort to get more information about the non-responding institutions we referred to an excellent study carried out by Alexander W. Astin of the American Council on Education, *Who Goes Where to College?*[5] Astin's study deals with almost exactly the same group of institutions as our own and lists each one with certain descriptive information. We found that data on all but nine of our non-respondents were listed, enabling us to analyze the schools which did not return our questionnaires. The non-responding schools proved to be statistically indistinguishable from other comparable American institutions in terms of Astin's variables, which describe the quality and orientation of each school and characteristics of its entering freshmen.

On the basis of these findings we concluded that the characteristics of non-responding colleges were essentially of a random nature and that the reasons given for not participating in the study probably did not mask a desire to conceal information about student freedom in these in-

[5] Alexander W. Astin, *Who Goes Where to College?* (Chicago: Science Research Associates, 1965).

stitutions. However, when an administration's attitude toward social research or questionnaires led college officials to refuse explicitly to participate, it seems reasonable to suppose that student freedom of expression on social issues might also be limited. In summary, failure to respond was remarkably limited for a questionnaire study of this type and probably did not significantly bias the results.

Interpretation of Findings

Our very high response rate and our finding of no systematic biases in the characteristics of schools returning questionnaires permit us to place confidence in the reported findings as representative of all the institutions included in our population. We took an additional precaution, however, to avoid making unwarranted generalizations from our findings. Statistical tests were applied to determine the significance of different proportions of respondents answering questions in given ways. Such tests are common to social scientists and our brief discussion of them below need not be reviewed by readers familiar with statistical methods, although they should note that we used two-tailed tests and adjusted for the finite population situation[6] according to the proportion of subgroup response as shown in Table 2. For readers unfamiliar with statistics some explanation of methods and conventions should assist their interpretation of the tabular presentation of data.

In most tables we report the percentage of respondents of the various categories of institutions answering questions in a given way. We asked of our data: Does a difference exist between the proportion of each group responding a particular way and the proportion of all schools responding the same way? If those invited to respond from all 1,000 institutions had completed and returned questionnaires, we would simply have had to examine the magnitude of the percentage figures to determine whether or not a real difference existed. Since all persons invited did not respond, we had to ask whether apparent differences could be explained away as artifacts of measurement, or whether the random response of schools deluded us and spuriously produced the appearance of a difference where in fact none existed.

[6] Following McNemar's reasoning, we accepted the rule that the standard error of a proportion should be decreased as the sample size becomes large relative to the number of schools in the population. See Quinn McNemar, *Psychological Statistics*, 2nd ed. (New York: John Wiley and Sons, 1955), pp. 99–100.

The hypothesis that apparent differences were the result of chance events was tested. Thus, in each table we note those differences which are statistically significant. We use asterisks as convenient symbols to express the fact of statistical significance: * to indicate significance at the .05 level and ** at the .01 level. To say that a difference between percentages is "significant at the .05 level" means that, if one were to take an infinite number of random samples of the same size from the same populations, a difference in percentages would be observed at least 95 times in 100 on the average; or, conversely, no difference between the proportions would be found in 5 or fewer of 100 samples. Thus, when a percentage is marked with a single asterisk considerable confidence can be placed in the statement that a real difference between percentages exist. Even greater confidence can be placed in percentages marked with a double asterisk because this symbol means that a difference would be found no fewer than 99 out of 100 times on the average. In tables where the actual numerical difference is not shown, the magnitude and direction of the difference between the specific category and all categories are determinable by inspection of the percentage figures. The reader will be well advised to consider especially those findings that are marked as statistically significant when interpreting the tables in this volume.

Statistical significance may or may not mean that a particular difference has "practical significance" for understanding the broader questions of student freedom. Thus, in the following pages we have sought to highlight and describe accumulations and patterns of findings which emerge from our analyses. The patterns and trends add weight to conclusions. From time to time we suggest what seem to us to be plausible hypotheses to account for data patterns. These are attempts on our part to weave separate strands into a meaningful fabric. We offer our interpretations both to answer why differences are found and to stimulate the reader to generate his own hypotheses about underlying causes for observed results. While interpretation is a very important element of the report, the reader should realize that our hypotheses represent only our best guesses to explain the data, and others may in the long run prove to have greater explanatory power. All our interpretations and hypotheses are subject to elaboration and confirmation or rejection by further research. Our purpose in this study is to delineate and describe, but social scientists should continue to seek answers to the "why's" asked by our data.

Now we ask the reader to join the search with us as we turn to examine evidence. How may we describe the atmosphere of colleges with regard to freedom of student expression? Are changes to be discovered on our campuses? Do college administrators espouse a principle of student freedom as relevant to their educational mission?

These and other questions are considered in the following chapter.

2 ⁓

An Atmosphere of Change

ONE fact emerges from a review of the conflicting reports concerning today's college students. Students are currently attracting more sustained attention than they have in many years. Some accounts portray them as immature and irresponsible rebels, others emphasize their deepening sense of social responsibility, and still others indicate that they are restless about their rights and responsibilities as students and citizens. In whatever light they are viewed, today's students no longer resemble the student generation of the fifties, generally characterized (probably with less than full accuracy) as "quiet."

In what ways and to what degree have students changed? Are they indeed more concerned with issues beyond the campus horizon? Is their expression of this concern easier to discern—are they louder and more visible? These are questions to which we have a multitude of answers from social commentators across the country. These observers are, however, often removed from campus life. We are interested in discovering how educators and students perceive changes in students on their own campuses. Further, what ideological commitment does the college administration have to the attainment of students' academic freedom? To answer this second question, we formulated a definition of students' academic freedom and asked presidents and deans to comment on it, for it seemed reasonable that increased clamor on any campus would somehow be related to the attitude of those who administer the policies of the institution.

The nature of the relationship between the extent of student unrest and the degree of administrators' commitment to the ideal of academic freedom has never been investigated, but speculation gives rise to several alternate hypotheses. An institution whose philosophy is essentially proscriptive might, by its rigidity, invite student rebellion. However, the reverse is also possible. One might discover little student agitation at the colleges where the administration is most opposed to freedom, either because students do not desire freedom or because the administration effectively stifles every expression of desire for more freedom. At the other extreme, do permissive institutions experience a great deal of student clamor? If so, does this indicate that students are increasingly using their opportunity to speak and participate freely or does it indicate that students are confused and restless when freedom is given them without limitations or guidelines for its use?

A significant relationship will be shown to exist between the institution's philosophy of academic freedom and the degree to which the institution is experiencing change in the climate of student expression. We shall return to this relationship after answering these fundamental questions: Do students show an increased desire to exercise academic freedom, and Do administrators approve of this desire?

Student Clamor

Attempting to determine the extent of student interest in controversial issues, we asked five questions of all respondents: (1) Are students on your campus currently addressing themselves *more* to "controversial" issues than they did two and one-half years ago? (2) Are they currently advocating more extreme positions on "controversial" issues? (3) Are they becoming more openly demonstrative in expressions of their viewpoints on "controversial" issues? (4) Has the number of students on your campus participating in activities designed to express their viewpoints on "controversial" issues increased noticeably during the past two and one-half years? (5) At the present time, approximately what percentage of students do you estimate participate in such activities?

The time period of two and one-half years (September 1961 to April 1964 when the questionnaires were mailed) was chosen since it was assumed to be recent enough to be remembered well yet long enough to

24

reveal major trends. In asking these questions we hoped to discover whether student interest in extracurricular, political freedom was growing rapidly. According to the responses of both students and administrators, students are experiencing a great awakening of interest in political and social issues. Although students are not very widely perceived as taking more extreme positions on controversial matters than they did in the past, on a majority of campuses more students are more openly expressing more views. Figure 3 indicates the presidents' views on these points.

Despite the fact that both students and administrators seem to see the campus as a place of increasing turmoil, the total number of active students remains surprisingly small. More than half of the presidents reported that fewer than 10 per cent of their students are engaging in these activities, 30 per cent said that the number is more than 10 per cent on their campuses, and 14 per cent did not make an estimate (see Figure 4). The small number of students concerned with the discussion of controversial issues may be discouraging at first glance because it implies that the large majority do not share these concerns. One student editor commented: "Fewer than five per cent [of the students are active, but this] is not to say that the number is negligible." And the

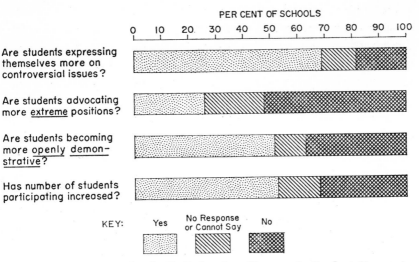

Figure 3. Percentage of Schools Indicating Changes in Student Expression during the Period from the Fall of 1961 to the Spring of 1964 (According to Presidents)

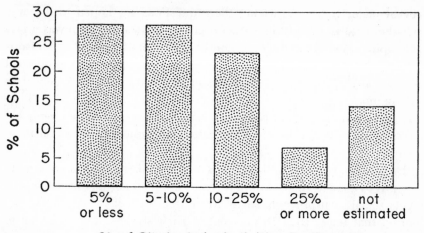

% of Students in Activities Designed to
Express Student Viewpoint

Figure 4. Percentage of Schools with Various Proportions of Students in Activities Designed to Express Student Viewpoints about Controversial Issues (According to Presidents)

student body president on another campus said that the number is "not especially large, but significant."

We are seeking to learn where student freedoms prevail and where campus administrators and faculty members are taking great interest in these freedoms. Is the current re-examination exclusively for the benefit of a small group of students? Do the majority of students simply not care? It is perhaps wise to question such an oversimplified conclusion as that the nonparticipation of the majority is "apathy." A president of a Catholic coeducational college stated bluntly, "Our students are too docile and not political enough." But in a lengthy and well-considered statement a dean of students, after completing the questionnaire, commented:

Our students are not as placid as this questionnaire might lead one to believe. However, perhaps because they are girls, they are more interested in University, city, and [state] affairs. They are members of [the State] Intercollegiate Student Association whose headquarters are on our campus. Student Government officials serve jointly on a committee with [another] University and the [city] Chamber of Commerce to promote the welfare of the city. They participate in the Model United Nations held each year at the University of [the state]. Right now Campus Government Association is engaged in completely rewriting their constitution, but it is being done without conflict or disagreement. They have discussed their ideas with me and with other faculty advisers and we are invited to sit in on all their deliberations. We have an excellent working relationship.

The above activities, the many and varied social activities, together with the high academic requirements leave them little time to become involved in protest movements. They know, too, that they will always be listened to and their suggestions considered fairly and objectively.

The dean of a small midwestern Catholic girls school was a bit more ambivalent when assessing the "apathy" of her students. She first described their awareness: "I believe that our students are reasonably well-informed about controversial issues. In many cases they would not be if the faculty was not alert to them. In my opinion, they do not read enough current news nor do they seem eager to watch TV newscasts." Then she seemed to doubt the accuracy of her assessment and commented: "Perhaps our students are somewhat apathetic to social problems, but I would like to think that their attitude is more that of inquiry rather than action at this stage of their education, and that opportunities to learn and form convietions are adequate."

From these and other notes on the questionnaires it seems likely that many students are active in political or social causes without generating noise on the campus or focusing their attention on issues which are controversial. Joining the Peace Corps and doing volunteer work in slums or hospitals are examples of this sort of activity. Also, students may be engaged in spirited debate on the issues of our time but in an informal manner rather than as participants in politically oriented student groups.

Our current inquiry does not seek justification from the number of students pressing for extension of their freedom. The changes that are even now taking place on many campuses would seem to have relevance for all students although only a few may be articulate enough to call our attention to their needs. It is even possible that students in a restrictive environment have not formulated these demands because they are unaware that an atmosphere of free and open inquiry might be desirable.

Where Is Student Clamor Greatest?

Respondents indicated that on a majority of campuses more students are becoming more articulate about controversial issues. The question now arises, which are those campuses? To answer this question we analyzed the responses by geographical region and by the ten-way classification of institutions described in Chapter 1.

Geographical analysis of the responses revealed that the increase in student interest in controversial issues has taken place more or less to the same extent across the country. However, when responses were classified according to the ten institutional categories some significant differences were observed. Figure 5 summarizes this analysis. Catholic universities, Catholic liberal arts colleges, and private universities perceived more change than did other types of schools, and technical institutions perceived less. Although there were some variations within the categories these four types of schools responded so differently from the others that statistically there is less than a 1 per cent probability that this happened by chance. Tentative explanations for these differences will be considered later.

Administrators' Ideological Commitment to Academic Freedom

Evidently students are taking an increasing interest in the controversial issues of our society. How do college administrators feel about this tendency when it is presented to them in the abstract? In general, *they approve.*

College presidents and deans of students were asked in our questionnaire to comment on the relevance of the following statement to the educational philosophy of their institution: "It has been suggested that an *essential part* of the education of *each student* is the freedom to hear, critically examine, and express viewpoints on *a range* of positions held and advocated regarding issues that divide our society." Few people in America oppose freedom; thus a question asking whether one is an advocate of freedom is likely to elicit a "yes." This statement of belief is worded strongly enough, however, so that we anticipated a number of respondents would qualify their agreement with the statement in significant ways.

The comments on this open-ended statement were classified into four categories: agreement, qualified agreement, restricted agreement, and disagreement. As Figure 6 shows, 72 per cent of the deans and 64 per cent of the presidents agreed with the statement of educational philosophy without any qualifications. The responses to this question were

28

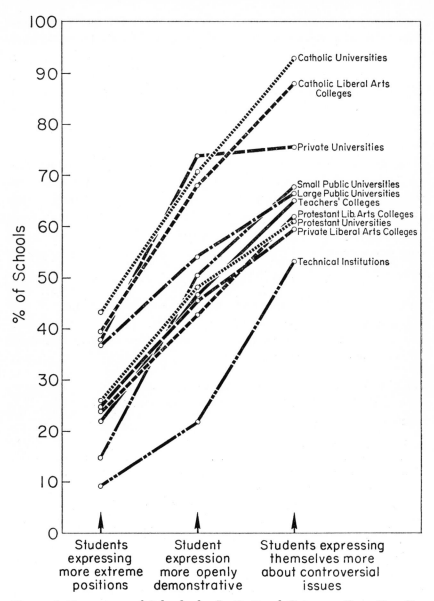

Figure 5. Percentage of Schools, by Institutional Category, Reporting Students To Be More Expressive than Before (According to Presidents)

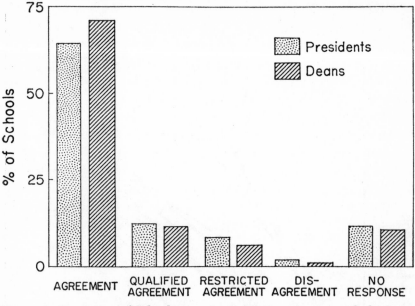

Figure 6. Percentage of Schools Agreeing to Various Degrees with the Statement That Student Freedom Is Relevant to Institutional Philosophy (According to Presidents and Deans of Students)

thoughtful and articulate. Here are excerpts from a few of the presidents and deans who expressed unqualified agreement with our statement:

It is one of the obligations of an institution of higher learning to create
an environment in which each student is free to hear and to express his
viewpoints on controversial contemporary issues as it is his same privilege to hear and express views about past issues in human society. The
college is not an intellectual morgue, devoted only to post-mortems.

Freedom of expression, regardless of viewpoint, is encouraged on this
campus, and it is considered to be an integral part of the educational
process.

I am a bit surprised by some of the questions herein raised. Students
on this free campus have never hesitated to express themselves on any
issue before the state, the nation, or world society. . . .

[Students have] taken real leadership on this campus and I feel at times
that they are in front of our faculty by some distance.

We encourage ferment and controversy, but it should be generated and

30

directed by students—not faculty sponsored. Growth comes out of controversy properly employed.

Not all of the administrators who agreed with the statement thought that controversy should be fomented deliberately, but none indicated in response to this abstract assertion that they would discourage student initiative in dealing with controversial issues.

Another group of responses, classified as "agreement," came from schools with specialized curricula where administrators said that they were personally committed to the philosophy of freedom, but expressed concern that their students lacked interest:

[This statement is] the philosophy, if not the practice, of our institution. In fact, as a college of science and engineering, it is often difficult to find a good hearing on political issues because a need for such hearings is not always strongly felt.

. . . this college is wholly teacher-preparatory. I have come to believe that those committed at an early age to teach are far more conservative than the general run of youth. Many of them feel it's prudent not to get too involved. We have, perhaps amazingly, never had any type of "demonstration." The *hottest* issue in eight years . . . was over the location of parking lots.

The responses classified as "qualified agreement" mentioned limitations of academic freedom rather than its benefits, prescribed a certain decorum or style for a speaker rather than accepting his natural manner, indicated the respondent was apprehensive that controversy would mar the contemplative atmosphere of the university, or mentioned that social action and strife should not submerge education. Such statements have a "yes, but . . ." character. They contain phrases such as "for the most part," "in general," and "I would tend to agree." Most of these respondents asserted that the principle of academic freedom was relevant but that it should be exercised responsibly. Twelve per cent of the presidents' and 11 per cent of the deans' responses were classified in this category. Statements of this position included the following:

Free inquiry is essential even if politically sensitive issues and people are involved . . . Sensation seeking is not always to be confused with free inquiry . . . Freedom of expression should be coupled with the responsibility to get the facts. This is the weakest point of student performance. They have to learn the difference between opinion, rumor, prejudice, and fact, and they must learn to prefer fact.

31

The quest for that knowledge which will free the student from the limitations of ignorance, prejudice and superstition must lead him down many avenues. The atmosphere of the institution must be such as to be conducive to this search. The process, however, must be orderly and the conduct of the freedom must be characterized by reason.

Freedom should be used to enable the student to make a choice. It should involve a responsible personal commitment to societal issues that can be changed by individual or group action. It should involve a set of values arrived at with discrimination and used as guiding principles. Freedom without commitment or responsibility is not an indication of maturity.

The admonition by many of these educators that freedom must be used "responsibly" might be taken to mean that students ought to be allowed "freedom" only so long as they use it precisely as the administrator thinks it should be used. However, the tenor of most of these answers indicates that this was probably not the intended meaning. These administrators seem willing to grant considerable freedom, including the freedom to make mistakes, but they also consider it their duty to teach students humane attitudes and to equip them with the tools of reason so that this freedom will not be abused but used to advantage.

Within the "qualified agreement" category the responses of some administrators contained two other types of qualifications. One was that it was difficult to apply this philosophy, the other that freedom should not be allowed to sully the institution's good name. The first is a recognition of the limitations imposed by the environment, which other administrators may simply have felt inappropriate to mention in their response to an abstract statement of educational philosophy. The second reflects a fear for loss of prestige or sources of funds—a concern which seems to be more prevalent at the smaller, less well known colleges.

One administrator, having expressed his essential agreement with the philosophy as stated, spoke of the difficulties of applying it, asserting that ". . . for those of an older generation, disagreement often seems to be akin to disloyalty—this, not from a desire to deter truth-seekers, but from an ingrained conservatism. In the long run this conservatism serves as a salutary balance, even while it irks the young . . .". At another institution, the president said, "We agree . . . although not to the extent that we will permit a student group or a student to undermine the institution with his views." In many other cases, administrators spoke of the views of local citizens, parents, or alumni as deterrents to a full implementation of the principles of freedom.

The responses placed in the third classification, "restricted agreement" (fewer than 10 per cent), were those in which although the respondent said he agreed his reservations seemed to outweigh his agreement. Most of these strong reservations were on religious grounds; assertions were made that students must accept a specific religious doctrine and that they ought not to be allowed to express disagreement on doctrinal issues, or to advocate positions contrary to accepted beliefs. Here are some examples of this position:

Our philosophy begins with certain basic assumptions that we do not hesitate to acknowledge. The nature of our institution assumes certain basic Christian principles. This framework has long been a part of the institution and a student accepts it when he comes.

Being a one-purpose (teacher education for Lutheran schools) institution, students are expected to conform generally to the viewpoints held by the church body. Freedom within this, on non-doctrinal issues, is permitted.

As a Catholic college there are fundamental concepts of natural law, dogma, and morals which would prevent this statement from being accepted in an absolute manner. In some matters it would be permissible to "express viewpoints," but not advocate them.

In addition to those who agreed with the statement of academic freedom, and those who agreed but expressed some degree of qualification or restriction, 4 per cent of the presidents and 1 per cent of the deans disagreed. One wrote, "As it now stands, the statement is not a working one, nor a sane one, nor a reasonable one." Other negative responses were somewhat more illuminating, and several contained articulate and thoughtful rationales for the restriction of academic freedom:

[Academic freedom is] relevant to public or state colleges and universities; *not* relevant (as in our case) to private denominational colleges or universities.

A philosophy of education based on absolutes provides the student with a sound foundation as a starting point and as a point of comparison. A student that is allowed to hear, examine and express viewpoints indiscriminately benefits neither himself nor his peer group.

The child is not left to drown if his first independent efforts [at swim-

ming] are unsuccessful. No beginner can be expected to debate success-
fully with Socrates, Dante, Newton or Karl Marx—even when it is only
an instructor wearing borrowed doctrines . . . at no time should we
give the impression that we subscribe to the thesis that there are no
certainties available. . . .

In summary, most of the presidents and deans agreed with an abstract
formulation of the principle of academic freedom, some of them lament-
ing that students did not seize the initiative in this matter. Others qualified their agreement with the statement that freedom should be exercised responsibly—that is, guided by the educated reason and conscience
of the individual. Some described the difficulties of implementing this
philosophy and others feared for the reputation of their institution were
its students not held in check. Many Christian educators found their
agreement restricted by their responsibility for inculcating a body of
dogma—if students choose to attend a religiously oriented school, these
college officials indicated, they must expect that academic freedom will
not extend to the basic tenets of the institution. A few respondents
found the statement anathema and said so, while others expressed disapproval on the grounds that students should be taught absolutes rather
than allowed to grapple, unaided, with the great problems of humanity.

The president and the dean of students of each institution tended to
share the same philosophy. This was verified by examining the differences between the president's response and the dean's response in each
institution. Figure 7 presents the results. At more than half of the schools
there was no disparity evident and at another 17 per cent presidents
and deans differed by no more than one category, e.g., the president
agreed without qualification while the dean expressed some qualification. In view of the philosophical differences which probably do exist
between the president and the dean this consistent result is quite remarkable. However, deans did show a slightly greater tendency to agree
with the statement than did presidents. Our own hypothesis to explain
this is that deans are generally in a better position than presidents to
detect the ways in which students develop intellectually by exercising
freedom of expression outside the classroom. Because they are in a
guidance relationship with students and observe the educational benefits of student expression, deans more frequently affirm the necessity of
student freedom.

Many presidents, while indicating essential agreement with the state-

34

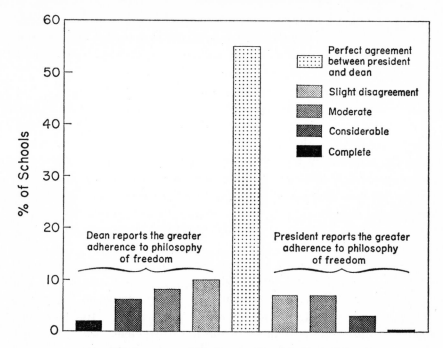

Figure 7. Congruity between Presidents' and Deans' Perceptions of the Relevancy of Student Freedom to Institutional Philosophy

ment, stressed the difficulties encountered in implementing policies that embody these principles and commented on the political and social forces impinging on their ability to enact student freedoms. These restraints are exerted by regents, legislators, faculty and students, alumni and parents, the local community, the press, ethnic units, and religious and pressure groups. These pragmatic presidents, while committed to a free forum as an ideal, occasionally insisted that they might sometimes have to prohibit an inflammatory speech or demonstration in order to pacify an intransigent legislature or a seriously fragmented board of trustees. In their effort to resolve conflicting pressures they sometimes felt it necessary to postpone or cancel debate—losing an occasional battle in order later to win the war.

Which institutions were strongest in their support of academic freedom and which were weakest? Analysis by geographical region revealed no significant differences except that slightly fewer administrators embrace the philosophy of freedom in the Northwest. A further analysis by type of institution according to our ten-way classification distinguished three groups of schools: Catholic schools, private universities and liberal arts colleges, and technical institutions. All other types of institutions subscribed to the principle of academic freedom to substantially the same extent.

At Catholic schools there was the least commitment to the formulation of student academic freedom. Within the total of responding presidents and deans 68 per cent expressed agreement with the statement, but at Catholic colleges and universities only 44 per cent agreed. At private universities and liberal arts colleges there was the greatest agreement with the proposition: at private universities 83 per cent of the presidents and deans agreed and at private liberal arts colleges 78 per cent agreed.

Technical institutions show a remarkably different pattern. A record 90 per cent of the deans subscribed to the statement while only 48 per cent of the presidents agreed with it—a highly significant difference. Thus, this group of deans appears to believe in academic freedom more than any other group of deans while their presidents are among the most skeptical of all presidents. In no other type of institution was a similar disparity found.

Student Clamor and Administrators' Commitment to Academic Freedom

In the opinion of our respondents student interest in controversial issues had grown unmistakably in the two and one-half years before the study, and the majority of administrators agree emphatically that students must, as part of the educational process, be free to examine divisive social issues. The greatest increase in student interest has been perceived in the Catholic schools and the private universities while the least change has been perceived in the technical institutions. Also, the greatest commitment to the abstract principle of academic freedom is found in the private universities and liberal arts colleges and the least is found in the Catholic schools. At technical institutions twice as many deans as presidents are committed to the principle. How can these patterns be explained?

The following hypotheses offer tentative explanations. At Catholic institutions, where student clamor is reportedly greatest, there is an avowed belief in certain fundamental precepts, and hence a commitment to the formulation of academic freedom as presented in the questionnaire cannot be complete. But the Roman Catholic Church is itself re-examining important doctrines, a phenomenon which apparently has swept students into the current of a controversy whose dimensions are international. The fact of general ferment in the Catholic Church contrasted with a traditional conservatism may have led Catholic college respondents to overestimate the increase in student expression of opinions about divisive issues.

At private universities and liberal arts colleges there is the strongest commitment to academic freedom. Also, an unusually great increase in student interest in controversial issues was perceived in the private universities although not in the private liberal arts colleges. It would seem that in private universities students are making use of existing freedoms while in private liberal arts colleges students either are less active or are not granted in practice the freedoms to which their administrators subscribe in principle. There may be no single explanation. Universities, because their social commitment may be more immediate, taking the form of engagement in government projects and social research, are more apt to be at the storm center of controversy than are the colleges. Therefore, the freedom of students to express themselves on a variety of issues may be greater at universities than at colleges because the tradition of academic freedom is more firmly established at these larger institutions. Only after examining the practices of freedom in detail in subsequent chapters will we be able to re-evaluate these hypotheses.

At technical institutions many respondents reported that their students are more interested in the difficult and exacting curriculum than in broad social issues. Thus the lack of increase in student interest in controversial issues may be easily explained and incidents of controverted student academic freedom may seldom arise. Because such incidents are few in number, the philosophical issue of academic freedom as a part of extracurricular education may seem an irrelevant one to the administrators, and thus discrepancies in outlook between a president and his dean may not need to be reconciled, and may even pass unperceived. This possibility throws further light on the remarkable consistency of other groups of presidents and deans. The degree to which a president's viewpoint coincides with that of his dean might indicate the degree to which the university's philosophy has been tested in practice.

In 1955 Lazarsfeld and Thielens[1] asked members of social science faculties across the nation whether students had changed. Their answer was yes. Their students, compared with those of a few years before, were more conservative, more cautious in their activities, and less willing to experiment with radical ideas. Ten years later the pendulum seems to have swung in the other direction. From colleges all over the nation our respondents reported that their students are increasingly involved in the discussion of controversial issues and are more willing to demonstrate this concern openly. While it was not generally the opinion of our respondents that students are more radical in their views it is evident that students were seen as having chosen more demonstrative techniques of expression to make their views known.

American college administrators adhere in principle to the ideal of academic freedom for students. Most administrators in our sample indicated that their universities subscribed without reservation to a strong and unequivocal definition of student rights. While their theoretical adherence to these ideals is impressive it is only one measure of the liberty accorded students in their extracurricular life. Are these freedoms really practiced? Do administrators act out their allegiance to freedom in the situations with which they are confronted every day?

We presented all the respondents at each institution with a list of topics, speakers, and situations, each of which was considered controversial to some degree. Did the university administrators reaffirm their dedication? Did three-fourths again indicate that their institutions are open to discussion of any controversial issue? When presented with a list of speakers who might be invited by student organizations, how often did respondents assert that students would be allowed to hear controversial and unpopular viewpoints? When presented with a list of situations upon which a judgment would have to be made, would administrators permit the exercise of the freedom which they praise in principle?

The answers to these questions, found in the following chapters, will indicate how much freedom American college students would probably be granted, if they, in fact, sought to exercise their freedoms fully.

---

[1] Paul F. Lazarsfeld and Wagner Thielens, Jr., *The Academic Mind: Social Scientists in a Time of Crisis* (Glencoe, Ill.: Free Press, 1958).

3 ✔

Free Discussion of Controversial Issues

MEMBERS of an earlier college student generation might well feel that
history is repeating itself as they observe students' quickening interest
in controversial issues, their deepening commitment to social reform,
and their awakening to the world around the campus. And today's ac-
tivists might be surprised to discover that their involvement in larger
issues is no innovation and may be but a pale imitation of their parents'
immersion in the campus political life of the thirties. At that time a host
of organizations emerged determined to translate every utopian dream
into reality. The hopes of many of these organizations were forgotten in
the years following World War II and students became silent on social
issues for many years.

Now students seem to have awakened from a twenty-year slumber
and are focusing their energy and enthusiasm on social, judicial, political, and economic reforms, and expressing interest in every vital issue
of the day. Dennis Shaul, a former president of the United States National Student Association, writes, "The signs of it [a political revival
among students] are everywhere: in the number of new campus political
organizations, in the proliferation of peace and civil rights groups, in
the number of new socio-political and political journals directed at the
student audience, and perhaps, most notoriously in the number of controversies which arise on the college campus over speaker bans and

other issues of academic freedom."[1] Although our data support Shaul in finding a reawakening of student interest in controversial issues, our queries about student organizations indicate that student participation in socially and politically controversial matters may be largely individual and unstructured, rather than channeled through formal student organizations. Many campuses simply do not have a wide range of student groups with social or political aims.

Before turning to the question of which issues are open for discussion by student organizations today, in order to determine the extent of freedom practiced in this area, we shall first discuss the nature of the organizations. A university's tolerance for freedom of speech can be judged better after discovering whether it has allowed or would allow the existence of the very organizations whose actions test this freedom. Our investigation was threefold. We attempted to determine what range of political organizations currently existed, where and on what types of campuses they would be permitted, and how much university control they must accept in order to gain official recognition from the institution. Answers to these questions will tell us *who* may discuss controversial issues—we shall then determine *what* may be discussed.

Where Are Student Political Organizations Active?

How many political groups exist on today's campuses? Respondents were asked to examine a list of sociopolitical clubs and to answer the following question: "Which, if any, of the following student organizations are active on your campus, and which, if any, probably would not be permitted?"

Table 3 presents the list of organizations and the percentage of schools indicating that the organization was active on their campus. The difficulties of compiling a list of political organizations were many, not only because so many different groups exist, but also because political clubs, in particular, tend to shield themselves behind an array of bewildering titles. In order to deal with this problem some organizations were given generic names (e.g., Student Communist Club, Student Conservative Club, and Students for Integration) so that each respondent could make an association with the corresponding clubs on his campus even though the local organization name might be quite differ-

[1] Dennis Shaul, "Student Political Movements: The Failure of Polarity," *New Generation,* Fall 1963.

ent. But when actual organizations were listed, such as the Student Peace Union or the Students for Democratic Society, it was not possible to circumvent this kind of confusion, and the high proportion of respondents who checked "cannot say," or did not respond at all, may indicate some uncertainty about the purposes of these organizations.

An attempt was made to span the political spectrum. In addition to the Young Republicans, the Student Conservative Club and the Young Americans for Freedom represent politically conservative elements. The Americans for Democratic Action, the Students for Democratic Society, the Young Socialist Alliance, and the Student Communist Club represent a range of left of center groups. Special cause-related groups are the Student Peace Union and the United World Federalists, both of which are active in arranging demonstrations for world peace; Students for Integration; and the Fair Play for Cuba Committee.

As Table 3 indicates, political organizations do not appear to be prominent in campus life. The only politically oriented organizations from the list which are active on more than half of the campuses are the Young Republicans and Young Democrats; they are active at about three-fourths of the schools. Conservative groups such as a Student Conservative Club or the Young Americans for Freedom, while not represented on most campuses, appear to be more prevalent than their liberal counterparts—groups such as the Americans for Democratic Ac-

Table 3. Percentage of Schools Reporting Student Organizations To Be Active on the Campus (According to Deans of Students and Student Body Presidents)

Organization	Deans of Students	Student Body Presidents	Difference
Young Republicans	74	73	1
Young Democrats	73	71	2
Student Conservative Club	17	18	1
Student Peace Union	9	10	1
Young Americans for Freedom	9	13	4*
Students for Integration	5	5	0
Americans for Democratic Action	5	5	0
World Federalist Club	4	3	1
Students for Democratic Society	3	3	0
Young Socialist Alliance	3	3	0
Fair Play for Cuba Committee	2	2	0
Student Communist Club	0.3	0.1	0.2

* The difference between deans and student body presidents is significant at the .05 level.

tion and the Students for Democratic Society, which appear on only 5 per cent and 3 per cent of the campuses, respectively. Socialist and Communist clubs are virtually not visible.

Which campuses have the greatest number and variety of student political organizations? Analysis of responses by institutional category indicates that the types of colleges whose administrators most frequently support the ideals of freedom are also the institutions which possess the greatest variety of organizations engaging in activity on controversial issues.

Analysis by Categories of Institutions

Table 4 shows which types of colleges have significantly more or fewer of each sociopolitical club than the average of all schools. Even the most popular political organizations are significantly underrepresented at some types of schools. While the Young Republicans and Young Democrats are found at the great majority of schools, they are represented at fewer of the Protestant colleges, technical institutions, teachers' colleges, and Catholic liberal arts colleges.

The four types of schools which possess the fewest of *all* types of political organizations are the teachers' colleges, the technical institutions, and the Protestant and Catholic liberal arts colleges. Nonsectarian universities, both private and public, have the greatest number of political organizations as well as the greatest range from extreme left to extreme right. Some extreme left groups are seldom found except at these schools. A Communist group is reported at 4 per cent of the large public universities as compared with less than 1 per cent of all schools. The Young Socialist Alliance and the Students for Democratic Society appear on about 30 per cent of these campuses as compared with 3 per cent nationally. But these are not the only organizations that are unusually well represented. Conservative groups, too, appear significantly more often at these types of institutions. For example, the Young Americans for Freedom have branches on 40 per cent of the large public university campuses and on 22 per cent of the private university campuses, whereas this organization is active in only 9 per cent of all schools.

We have already noted that politically conservative clubs are generally better represented on campuses than are the politically liberal groups. This disproportion is especially marked in technical institutions where liberal political groups are virtually nonexistent and in the

Table 4. Percentage of Schools, by Institutional Category, Reporting Student Organizations To Be Active on the Campus (According to Deans of Students)

Organization	Universities					Colleges					
	Large Public	Small Public	Private	Protestant	Catholic	Private	Protestant	Catholic	Teachers'	Technical	All Categories
Young Republicans	100**	89**	87**	91**	81*	74	70*	61**	69*	69	74
Young Democrats	100**	89**	89**	91**	81*	71	66*	61**	70	66	73
Young Americans for Freedom	40**	16**	22**	18*	7	3**	4**	6*	1**	3*	9
Student Conservative Club	47**	16	33**	14	44**	20	10**	14*	7**	7*	17
Student Peace Union	58**	8	22**	5	0**	18**	1**	0**	3**	0**	9
Students for Integration	18**	5	13**	0*	4	5	1**	3*	4	0*	5
Americans for Democratic Action	27**	2*	20**	9*	4	3	1**	2**	2**	0*	5
World Federalists	22**	5	9**	0*	4	0**	1**	3	3	0*	4
Students for Democratic Society	27**	3	9**	5	0*	3	0**	0**	0**	0	3
Young Socialist Alliance	29**	0**	7**	0*	0*	4	0**	0**	1*	0	3
Fair Play for Cuba Committee	16**	2	7**	0	0	1	0*	0**	1	0	2
Communist Club	4**	0	0	0	0	0*	0*	0*	0*	0	0.3

* This percentage is significantly different from the percentage for all categories at the .05 level.
** This percentage is significantly different from the percentage for all categories at the .01 level.

smaller institutions, such as small public universities and liberal arts colleges. It is interesting to note, for example, that no Socialist club is reported to be active in any small public university but 29 per cent of large public universities report a Socialist group active on campus. The larger the school, of course, the more apt it is to have a greater number of organizations of all kinds, but it is apparent that the large schools reflect the greater balance of political views as well. It is not clear whether this is because size increases independence from conservative forces in the community, because liberalism increases with the size of the school, or because smaller schools attract more conservative students. The explanations for some of these trends may become evident when other measures are applied to these schools.

Some findings regarding Catholic schools bear special mention. Catholic universities report student Conservative Clubs on 44 per cent of their campuses, an unusually high percentage when compared with the national proportion of 17 per cent. This fact, coupled with the paucity of liberal groups, suggests that Catholic institutions are bulwarks of conservatism, as does the fact that Catholic liberal arts colleges reported almost as many student Conservative Clubs as the average, but significantly fewer of all other types of clubs than the average for all schools.

As we have said, only the Young Republicans and Young Democrats exist on most campuses. The two conservative organizations—the Student Conservative Club and the Young Americans for Freedom—are found on fewer than 20 per cent of the campuses, and all the others are reportedly present at fewer than 10 per cent of the institutions, most of them at only 3 or 4 per cent. The fewest organizations exist at technical institutions and teachers' colleges—perhaps because their specialized curricula draw attention away from controversial political issues—and at the sectarian liberal arts colleges, where small size and religious orientation may discourage the free formation of student political groups.

What else may explain the absence of these groups? Where no organizations exist to provide an outlet for expression, is the administration exerting a subtle form of suppression by discouraging the establishment of these organizations? Are students simply not interested in the controversial societal issues to which these organizations are likely to address themselves? Or are students finding other ways of expressing their concern for these matters? These questions await interpretation in

44

the light of respondents' answers to our second question, Where would these organizations probably not be permitted?

Where Would Student Organizations Not Be Permitted?

In Table 5 we see how deans and student body presidents responded to this question. Comparison of these data with Table 3 reveals first of all that the organizations deemed most acceptable are those most often found on campuses. This is hardly surprising. But closer examination of these tables indicates that students, as much as they have clamored for more freedom, have not begun to use the freedom that appears to be already available to them. For example, 3 per cent of the schools would probably not permit the Students for Democratic Society to organize. This means that since this organization is active on only 3 per cent of our campuses, an overwhelming 94 per cent of the schools neither have such a group on campus nor report serious overt objection to the establishment of one. Again and again there appears wide but unutilized freedom to form sociopolitical organizations, even the more unpopular ones. The Young Socialist Alliance, for example, is represented in only 3 per cent of the institutions but students could if they wished attempt to organize on another 72 per cent of the campuses, according to deans, and on 55 per cent according to student president respondents.

Analysis by institutional category reveals, as shown in Table 6, that

Table 5. Percentage of Schools Reporting That Various Student Organizations Would Probably Not Be Permitted (According to Deans of Students and Student Body Presidents)

Organization	Deans of Students	Student Body Presidents	Difference
Student Communist Club	57	66	9**
Fair Play for Cuba Committee	28	38	10**
Young Socialist Alliance	25	42	17**
Students for Integration	8	9	1
Student Peace Union	7	6	1
Young Americans for Freedom	6	5	1
Americans for Democratic Action	5	5	0
World Federalist Club	4	6	2
Students for Democratic Society	3	3	0
Student Conservative Club	2	2	0
Young Republicans	2	2	0
Young Democrats	2	2	0

** The difference between deans and student body presidents is significant at the .01 level.

Table 6. Percentage of Schools, by Institutional Category, Reporting That Student Organizations Would Probably Not Be Permitted (According to Deans of Students)

Student Organization	Universities					Colleges					
	Large Public	Small Public	Private	Prot-estant	Cath-olic	Private	Prot-estant	Cath-olic	Teachers'	Tech-nical	All Cat-egories
Young Republicans	0*	0*	0*	0	0	0**	1	8**	1	0	2
Young Democrats	0*	0*	0*	0	0	0**	1	8**	1	0	2
Conservative Club	0*	2	2	0	0	3	1	7**	3	0	2
Student Peace Union	0**	5	2**	0**	15**	7	6	14**	7	0*	7
Young Americans for Freedom	0**	2**	0**	0**	15**	9*	2**	14**	8	10	6
Students for Integration	2**	5*	2**	0**	7	10	9	5*	13**	10	8
Americans for Democratic Action	0**	3	2*	9*	7	4	2**	13**	3**	0*	5
World Federalists	0**	2	2	5	4	5	4	6*	4	7	4
Students for Democratic Society	0**	3	2	0*	4	4	2	8**	7**	0	3
Young Socialist Alliance	2**	11**	2**	9**	44**	19**	20*	62**	26	21	25
Fair Play for Cuba Committee	11**	24	7**	9**	52**	19**	24*	52**	30	21	28
Communist Club	33**	46**	24**	55	81**	37**	58	89**	61	66	57

* This percentage is significantly different from the percentage for all categories at the .05 level.
** This percentage is significantly different from the percentage for all categories at the .01 level.

46

some types of schools provide an atmosphere much more conducive to the formation of these groups than do others.

Among Catholic liberal arts colleges almost all the organizations are less acceptable than they would be elsewhere. Even the Young Republicans and Young Democrats would probably not be permitted by 8 per cent of these deans. Fourteen per cent of them would permit neither the liberal Student Peace Union nor the conservative Young Americans for Freedom. And more than half of these deans would reject the three most controversial groups.

The greatest tolerance is shown by the large public universities and the private universities, both of which reportedly would grant permission significantly more often than average for the establishment of student political organizations. None of the deans from large public universities would oppose two-thirds of the listed groups, and in reference to the other four groups they expressed opposition significantly less often than average. For example, a Socialist group would be discouraged by 25 per cent of all deans but by only 2 per cent of the deans from large public universities.

Two facts emerge. The presence of these groups is related to the institution's size and, not surprisingly, to the administrators' permissiveness toward these groups. The types of schools which have the fewest organizations also would permit them least often. Secondly, students have many opportunities to form political groups even in the Catholic liberal arts colleges, the least permissive type of institution. Very few of these kinds of organizations exist in Catholic colleges yet their students could, if they wished, form many of these groups.

Congruity of Response

The slight, but decided, tendency for student body presidents to view the present status of student freedom with greater alarm than administrators is apparent in many areas of this investigation, but nowhere more strikingly than in their estimates of which organizations would not be permitted on campus (see Table 5). Nine per cent more students than deans reported that their administrations would not permit a Communist group on campus; 10 per cent more of the students said this of the Fair Play for Cuba Committee; and 17 per cent more students than deans reported that their administration would discourage a branch of the Young Socialist Alliance.

Where is this disagreement occurring? Table 7 shows that it takes place to some degree at almost all types of schools. Students generally envision greater opposition to establishing student political groups than administrators say they would exert. Disagreement between the dean and student president is *least* at the least permissive type of school, the Catholic liberal arts college. Sixty-two per cent of deans and the same percentage of students agree that a Young Socialist Alliance would not be permitted; students at these schools are apparently accurate judges of their administrations. Disagreement is most pronounced in the Protestant schools. Looking again at the Young Socialist Alliance, we find that 9 per cent of the deans of Protestant universities reported that such a group would probably not be permitted, but 50 per cent of the student presidents thought the group would not be permitted. Again, in Protestant liberal arts colleges, 20 per cent of the deans would not permit its formation; and 50 per cent of the students thought their deans would not allow it. Table 7 reveals that similar incongruities appear with reference to a Communist Club and the Fair Play for Cuba Committee. Student presidents in Protestant schools regard their universities as very much less permissive than do the deans. In view of the fact that Protestant institutions, according to deans, are not less permissive than the average of all institutions for the formation of such groups, it appears that the students may be misjudging their administrators. Perhaps many of these administrators wish to appear much more permissive than they really would be. However, it is clear that students at many Protestant schools do not consider their administrators to be permissive about group establishment. Perhaps students have not tested their institutions enough to have learned where their actual limits are—and if this is the case, they may be surprised to learn that they have more freedom than they anticipate.

University Recognition

Assume that students wish to establish a campus political organization and the administration has indicated that it has no objection. We wanted to determine to what extent a group might forfeit its autonomy when it seeks official university recognition. Do universities curtail a group's freedom of speech without denying its right to exist? Our data indicate that universities indeed retain this power; whether they use it to control student expression will be considered later in this chapter.

48

Table 7. Percentage of Schools, by Institutional Category, Reporting That Student Organizations Would Probably Not Be Permitted (According to Deans of Students and Student Body Presidents)

	Universities					Colleges					
Organization	Large Public	Small Public	Private	Protestant	Catholic	Private	Protestant	Catholic	Teachers'	Technical	All Categories
Young Socialist Alliance											
Deans of students	2	11	2	9	44	19	20	62	26	21	25
Student body presidents	13	27	18	50	52	30	50	62	50	38	42
Difference	11*	16*	16**	41**	8	11	30**	0	24**	17	17**
Fair Play for Cuba Committee											
Deans of students	11	24	7	9	52	19	24	52	30	21	28
Student body presidents	20	25	16	55	63	24	42	56	40	34	38
Difference	9	1	9	46**	11	5	18**	4	10	13	10**
Communist Club											
Deans of students	33	46	24	55	81	37	58	89	61	66	57
Student body presidents	40	51	33	59	89	47	77	91	67	66	66
Difference	7	5	9	4	8	10	19**	2	6	0	9**

* The difference between the deans of students and student body presidents is significant at the .05 level.
** The difference between the deans of students and student body presidents is significant at the .01 level.

49

Colleges also have the means for limiting this or any other student activity.

At 10 per cent of the institutions groups are permitted to exist and function without official recognition. Only at these schools may student organizations be considered autonomous—the other institutions grant varying degrees of freedom at the university's discretion. What does official recognition entail? Of the institutions requiring official recognition, 95 per cent must approve the organization's constitution or purposes; 81 per cent require that an adviser be chosen—but only 26 per cent allow the student organization to choose its own adviser—and 28 per cent of schools require a period of probation. Nearly half of the institutions requiring a period of probation specify six months to a year and one-fourth report no specific length of probation. A long or indefinite period of probation could conceivably be a powerful tool in the hands of an administration anxious to render a potentially troublesome organization harmless, and approval of an organization's charter could possibly necessitate such major changes that the organization would forsake its initial purpose for university recognition. The faculty sponsor could be chosen so as to dampen the organization's spirits and impinge on its freedom of activity. But one cannot conclude that the university is using its traditional control privilege in these ways; our data merely identify possible channels of control. Most universities require approval of a group's constitution or charter, the selection of an adviser, and a period of probation.

Universities may or may not be curbing the formation of campus organizations. But once a group exists, how limited is the freedom of its members to espouse a specific position?

Which Topics May Student Groups Discuss?

The precise interpretation of the intent and meaning of the free speech clause in the First Amendment is determined by the federal courts and will not be considered here. However, some general distinctions made by the courts in terms of the substance, method, time, place, and purpose of free expression are relevant to our discussion. Freedom of speech generally means the right to provide information, to express a viewpoint, to advocate a viewpoint, or to advocate action as a consequence of holding a particular position. Freedom to express a viewpoint may mean, for example, the right to play the devil's advocate by

50

delineating one side of an issue, not necessarily from personal conviction, but for the purposes of teaching or exposition. Freedom to advocate a viewpoint implies the right to state a conviction as one's own and to try to convince others of its validity or utility. Freedom to advocate action suggests not only winning others to one's point of view but also convincing them that some program of action should be undertaken. Methods of expression range from the private expression of opinions through public expression (by petitioning, making speeches, or distributing pamphlets), to mass picketing or demonstration by organized groups. Here we are concerned with the substance and purpose of student expression: with the right of a student organization to express, in public, its convictions, even if unpopular, and to try to convince others of the merits of such convictions or to advocate action believed to be necessary.

Each of the respondents in our study was presented with a list of fourteen controversial topics and asked whether "student organizations on your campus holding 'unpopular' viewpoints could *publicly express* their positions." Three alternative responses were offered for each topic. These response choices were "unpopular viewpoints could be expressed," "cannot say," and "the administration would question the advisability of expressing unpopular viewpoints."

The ambiguity of "advisability questioned" was deemed preferable to the clear negative, "the viewpoint could not be expressed," for two reasons. First, we reasoned, administrators might be unwilling to class themselves as enemies of freedom by categorically denying the right to speak on the issue in question. Thus, even if in some cases they would permit students to speak on a topic they would be inclined to check "advisability questioned," if they would not allow its expression under most conditions. Second, administrators probably do not usually think in such absolute terms. They would rather persuade than prohibit and the term "advisability questioned" suggests an informal, reasoned review of the advisability of publicly expressing certain views—a procedure which might well produce as effective a check on student speech as a clear prohibition. Hence, we expected "advisability questioned" to elicit a larger and more accurate negative response than a stronger statement.

The fourteen topics presented to the respondents were chosen from a roster of more than one hundred issues subject to current controversy.

Since certain regions and certain types of schools were assumed to be especially sensitive to specific issues, an effort was made to select topics which were subjects of debate across the country and at a wide range of schools. In this way we hoped to avoid characterizing a school as "free" simply because we had neglected to include the issues which were taboo in that type of institution; or, on the other hand, characterizing a school as "restricted" because we included too many selectively taboo issues. Already some of the issues which were controversial when the questionnaires were constructed have become dated and arouse little interest, but we are concerned with the freedom to discuss currently divisive issues rather than with the specific issues themselves. While the issues may change, we assumed the freedom or lack of freedom to discuss issues would tend to remain. Intuitively, an assumption regarding stability of an institutional level of freedom seemed warranted.

The topics were as follows:
1. Laws Prohibiting Interracial Marriage
2. U.S. Participation in the World Court
3. One Bible for All Christians
4. Public Library Censorship
5. Total Military Disarmament
6. Abolition of Prayers in Public Schools
7. Admission of Red China to the U.N.
8. Sale of U.S. Farm Products to Russia or Soviet Satellites
9. Abolition by Catholics of Index of Forbidden Books
10. Abolition of the House Un-American Activities Committee
11. Local Fair Housing Legislation
12. Jail Sentences for Conscientious Objectors
13. Federal Aid to Yugoslavia
14. U.S. Dissemination of Birth Control Information to Underdeveloped Countries

As we have seen, most administrators believe in freedom of expression for students. This commitment is typified by the remarks of one president: "Freedom of expression, regardless of viewpoint, is encouraged on this campus, and it is considered to be an integral part of the educational process." Responses to the list of specific topics indicate that this commitment is generally met in practice. The data indicate that students on most campuses are, in fact, granted the right to speak their minds on controversial social issues. Figure 8 shows that, according to

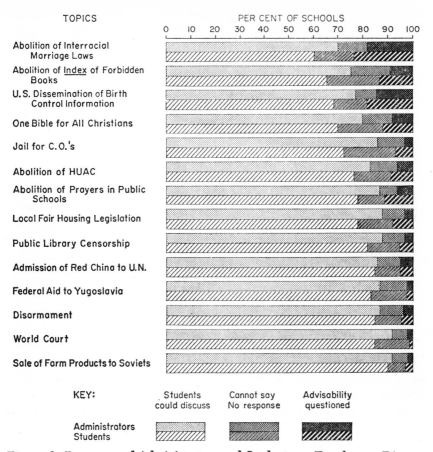

Figure 8. Responses of Administrators and Students on Freedom to Discuss Fourteen Topics

students and administrators alike, each topic could be freely discussed on most campuses. The fourteen topics have been arranged in the graph in order of controversiality, from most to least controversial, according to the percentage of respondents indicating that views on the issues could be expressed.

Each of the topics, with the exception of the four most controversial, would be acceptable for discussion by students in 80 per cent or more of the institutions. Figure 9 restates the findings in another way, in answer to this question: If all topics could be discussed on a majority of campuses, are the colleges which will permit free discussion of one issue the

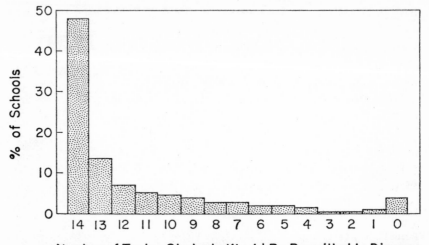

Figure 9. Percentage of Schools Indicating Number of the Fourteen Topics Students Would Be Permitted to Discuss (According to Presidents)

same colleges which will permit free discussion of the others? This is apparently the case, for, as Figure 9 indicates, all of the topics, even the most controversial, could be discussed in nearly half (48 per cent) of the institutions and unpopular viewpoints on ten or more of the issues could be expressed in 79 per cent of institutions. There is a basis for the conclusion that about 80 per cent of our institutions are open to discussion of all but the four most explosive of the listed issues.

Congruity of Response

Although students and administrators tend to agree that there is widespread freedom to discuss these issues further examination of Figure 8 reveals that students perceived less freedom on their campuses than did administrators. Looking more closely at the kinds of issues concerning which incongruity appears, one finds that although student answers to all items were more negative, they are especially more negative in response to the three most controversial issues. Fewer students than administrators are willing to concede that student groups would be permitted to advocate unpopular views—a difference of 10 per cent. The direction of this discrepancy again tends to confirm the hypothesis that in the struggle to increase their freedom students may attempt to appear more oppressed, and administrators more permissive, than they really are. Although these differences are statistically significant the fact remains that they are not large. Perhaps the true measure of freedom is somewhere between the conflicting contentions of students and administrators. Certainly, there does exist substantial freedom for student organizations publicly to express unpopular viewpoints on the nation's campuses.

A Closer Look at the Issues

The four topics on which schools would be most reluctant to permit discussion are interracial marriage, abolition by Catholics of the Index of Forbidden Books, dissemination of birth control information by the United States, and one Bible for all Christians. From 27 to 34 per cent of the schools were unwilling to commit themselves to permit public discussion by students of these issues, all of which have religious overtones. Other religious issues are also among the more controversial. For example, one-fifth of the respondents were unwilling to say that prayer in public schools and jail sentences for conscientious objectors could be discussed.

A closer examination of the responding institutions reveals that, as indicated in Table 8, all issues may be discussed with greater freedom in large public universities, and in private universities and liberal arts colleges, than in other types of schools. The most restrictive schools are the teachers' colleges and the Catholic liberal arts colleges.

Institutions with religious sponsorship, in general, do not appear to be more sensitive to religious issues than are nonsectarian schools. Catholic universities for example are as permissive as average with regard to these topics, as are the Protestant universities and liberal arts colleges. The high degree of restrictiveness of teachers' colleges is not limited to issues of a religious nature—which might be expected in publicly supported schools—but as in Catholic liberal arts colleges this restrictiveness extends to most topics, regardless of the religious or political nature of the issue. This general finding runs counter to the statements from presidents and deans of religiously affiliated schools (noted in Chapter 2) to the effect that religious orientation necessitates special caution in the treatment of doctrinal issues. The only issue to which responses confirm the administrators' views is dissemination of birth control information. Catholic schools in which this is clearly a doctrinal

Table 8. Percentage of Respondents, by Institutional Category, Reporting That Students Would Be
Permitted to Express Unpopular Viewpoints about Various Topics

Topics	Universities					Colleges					All Categories
	Large Public	Small Public	Private	Protestant	Catholic	Private	Protestant	Catholic	Teachers'	Technical	
Abolition of interracial marriage laws	76**	64	81**	54**	70	72*	61*	62*	60**	64	66
Abolition of Index of Forbidden Books	82**	70	80**	68	71	77**	70	73	54**	65	70
U.S. dissemination of birth control information	90**	81**	88**	77	42**	84**	82**	32**	72	74	72
One Bible for all Christians	88**	74	86**	72	69	83**	78*	65**	65**	74	73
Jail for conscientious objectors	89**	82	90**	77	82	87**	80	67**	73**	83	79
Abolition of House Un-American Activities Committee	90**	83*	90**	79	80	84*	79	74**	70**	78	79
Abolition of prayers in public schools	92**	86	92**	77	75*	88**	83	72**	80	82	82
Local fair housing legislation	92**	84	89*	84	90**	85	80	81	77**	81	82
Public library censorship	91**	86	93**	80	84	89**	84	78**	82	86	84
Admission of Red China to United Nations	96**	88	94**	84	88	88	86	78**	82*	84	85
Federal aid to Yugoslavia	93**	88	91**	87	89	88*	84	78**	80*	85	84
Total military disarmament	92**	84	92**	89	86	90**	89*	78**	81*	84	85
U.S. participation in the World Court	94**	91	93*	85	90	91	89	85	84**	89	88
Sale of farm products to Soviet satellites	96**	95*	94	93	96*	92	91	87**	88*	85*	91

* This percentage is significantly different from the percentage for all categories at the .05 level.
** This percentage is significantly different from the percentage for all categories at the .01 level.

issue are much less frequently permissive than others. The presidents and deans, however, implied that students would be accorded freedom of speech concerning nonreligious issues. Nevertheless our data indicate that in *most cases* it is not the content of the issue which is the determining factor. Schools which would not permit student expression on religious issues also tend not to permit student discussion of other issues.

Table 9. Percentage of Respondents, by Geographical Region, Reporting Students Would Be Permitted to Express Unpopular Viewpoints about Various Topics

Topics	New England	Middle Atlantic	North Central	North Western	Southern	Western	All Regions
Abolition of interracial marriage laws	77**	72**	67	72	49**	66	66
Abolition of Index of Forbidden Books	74	74*	69	70	67	64	70
U.S. dissemination of birth control information	74	69	72	78*	74	69	72
One Bible for all Christians	75	76	76**	75	72	72	73
Jail for conscientious objectors	79	83**	77*	85*	78	80	79
Abolition of House Un-American Activities Committee.	82	85**	79	78	73**	80	79
Abolition of prayers in public schools...	85	84	82	86	80	83	82
Local fair housing legislation	86	85	82	86	78*	86	82
Public library censorship	89*	88*	82*	84	85	84	84
Admission of Red China to United Nations	88	89**	86	88	82	78*	85
Federal aid to Yugoslavia	86	88*	84	87	82	82	84
Total military disarmament	88	89**	85	86	83	84	85
U.S. participation in the World Court ..	90	90	88	90	87	88	88
Sale of farm products to Soviet satellites	91	92	92	92	88*	88	91

* This percentage is significantly different from the percentage for all regions at the .05 level.

** This percentage is significantly different from the percentage for all regions at the .01 level.

It seems that it is not so much the issue at stake which is controversial; it is the freedom of speech itself.

Table 9 shows generally that institutions in the middle Atlantic states are relatively more open than are those in the South and West. Regional variations become more striking, however, on consideration of individual topics. If we examine the most divisive issue, interracial marriage laws, we observe that New England and the middle Atlantic states are significantly more free than average and that the South, predictably enough, is significantly more restrictive.

Summary

Most schools would allow student organizations to express unpopular viewpoints on controversial issues.

Religious topics would be approached with the greatest caution. Thirty-four per cent of respondents were unwilling to say that the most controversial issue, interracial marriage, could be discussed. The four most controversial topics, all of a religious nature, may be discussed in from 66 to 73 per cent of institutions. Thus, while a majority of institutions would permit free discussion of these issues a considerable minority have reservations.

When issues are of a social or political nature many more respondents indicate that students would be allowed to express unpopular views. Seventy-nine per cent of all schools would allow discussion of all but the four most controversial issues.

Those institutions which would be most apt to consider issues too controversial for students to handle are the Catholic liberal arts colleges and the teachers' colleges, both of which would hesitate before permitting their students to express themselves concerning religious and political issues alike.

It is uncertain just what forms hesitation to permit expression may take, but it is clear that almost all universities have reserved for themselves the right to intervene in the formation and operation of student organizations. An organization's charter and purposes are subject to university approval, and a faculty sponsor is usually required to oversee group activities. No colleges appear to allow so much freedom to students that a group's activities are not known to the administration through official channels.

Student groups are accorded freedom to discuss controversial topics at many schools, but most of them have few student action organizations and especially many lack those of radical persuasion. Although these groups do not exist on most campuses, administrators are not necessarily unwilling to tolerate them.

The general findings vary widely among different types of schools. Size or size-related variables appear to be major determinants of permissiveness. Larger schools generally, and those which are nonsectarian, appear to allow groups to form and express their views more often than the national average. Large public universities and private universities have many more student political organizations than the average for all schools, and also are significantly more willing to tolerate the addition of new groups, and to grant students freedom to discuss and publicly espouse unpopular views concerning controversial issues. Small public universities, on the other hand, have fewer politically oriented groups than do the large public universities and are relatively less willing to permit students in the organizations to express their views. Similarly, Catholic universities are about as permissive as the national average for freedom of discussion, but the smaller Catholic liberal arts colleges are significantly less so.

Protestant institutions are exceptions to this generalization. Respondents at both universities and liberal arts colleges report average permissiveness. But students at these schools are much more likely to report their administrators' permissiveness to be less than the administrators admit. Although we have noted a consistent tendency for students to perceive less freedom than the administrators do, Protestant students' responses were most discrepant from their administration in estimating whether groups would be allowed on campus, and in assessing permissiveness on actual issues.

A high degree of congruity exists in the least permissive institutions, the Catholic liberal arts colleges, in which student respondents apparently are not in doubt about the limits of their freedom.

Teachers' colleges and Catholic liberal arts colleges follow a similar pattern. One finds few organizations of a controversial nature on their campuses and they are significantly less willing than average to tolerate public debate on socially divisive issues. Catholic liberal arts colleges, moreover, are much less willing to tolerate the appearance of such organizations on campus. In these schools administrative reluctance to permit such groups to form and speak out on controversial issues may explain their scarcity.

In technical institutions the climate appears to be much more favorable for freedom of speech although these schools report almost as few political organizations as teachers' and Catholic colleges. But the lack of political groups on these campuses is apparently not due so much to the intolerance of the administration as to the students' lack of interest in sociopolitical affairs.

In the previous chapter we showed that most administrators believed in student academic freedom. Here we have shown that most schools permit considerable freedom of speech for student organizations. Now let us consider, in the next chapter, whether administrators extend their permissiveness to the invitation of controversial off-campus speakers.

4 ⁄

Invitation of Speakers on Controversial Issues

No single issue in the continuing debate over academic freedom for students has aroused more recent attention than the invitation of off-campus speakers. Students state their platform:

U.S. National Student Association supports the right to hear in live confrontation an off-campus speaker enunciate any opinion, regardless of its public popularity and regardless of the speaker's political beliefs or associations, his intellectual merits, or the possibility of causing a public disturbance.[1]

The American Association of University Professors backs them up:

Any person who is presented by a recognized student organization should be allowed to speak on a college or university campus. Institutional control of the use of campus facilities by student organizations for meetings and other organizational purposes should not be employed as a device to censor or prohibit controversial speakers or the discussion of controversial topics. The only controls which may be imposed are those required by orderly scheduling of the use of space.[2]

Finally, the American Civil Liberties Union supports the student position:

[1] *Student Dimensions, Codification of Policy of the United States National Student Association* (Philadelphia, Pa.: U.S.N.S.A., 1963–64), p. 115.
[2] American Association of University Professors, Committee "S," "Statement on Faculty Responsibility for the Academic Freedom of Students," *A.A.U.P. Bulletin,* Vol. 50, No. 3 (September 1964), p. 255.

Students should be accorded the right to assemble, to select speakers and to discuss issues of their choice. When a student organization wishes to invite an outside speaker it should give sufficient notice to the college administration. The latter may properly inform the group's leaders of its views in the matter but should leave the final decision to them. Permission should not be withheld because the speaker is a controversial figure. It can be made clear to the public that an invitation to a speaker does not necessarily imply approval of his views by either the student group or the college administration. Students should enjoy the same right as other citizens to hear different points of view and draw their own conclusions. At the same time, faculty members and college administrators may if they wish acquaint students with the nature of the organizations and causes that seek to enlist student support.[3]

These statements do not describe the situation that exists on most campuses today. Indeed, in the absence of data it has been far from clear what present policies regarding off-campus speakers exist, or how decisions have been made regarding invitations to these men.

Before turning to an analysis of the practices currently in effect at colleges, let us consider certain aspects of the off-campus speaker problem in order to understand just why this manifestation of the debate over student freedoms has attracted the most attention, and the most heated polemics.

Universities have traditionally served as public forums. The college platform has been a favorite place to launch many of our society's most profound visions, far-reaching programs, and, sometimes, most bitter attacks. The preference of speakers for the university platform reflects society's recognition of the dignity of the academic atmosphere, its traditions of free speech and fair play, and the respect which society's leaders have for college students and faculty. Winston Churchill delivered his famous "Iron Curtain" speech in 1946 at Westminster College in Fulton, Missouri. Senator Joseph McCarthy often used the college forum, as did the late President Kennedy and the 1964 Republican nominee Barry Goldwater. Advocates of free love, free land, and free spending have spoken to college audiences, as have atheists, agnostics, Paul Tillich, and Karl Barth. John Birchers and Communists, Madame Nhu and Margaret Chase Smith, Harry Belafonte and Governor George Wallace have spoken at one or another of our colleges. It was at Syracuse Uni-

[3] *Academic Freedom and Civil Liberties of Students in Colleges and Universities* (New York, N.Y.: American Civil Liberties Union, 1963), p. 7.

versity that President Johnson first spelled out American policy concerning Vietnam.

Because views expressed on the campus by public figures extend beyond the campus in their impact, the proper use of this platform is a source of discussion and sometimes division and discontent among students, faculty, trustees, legislators, parents, alumni, contributors, citizens, and community groups.

Also, the right of a student organization to invite an off-campus speaker involves a number of considerations that did not arise in connection with the issue of free speech. One of these is the basic question of the students' freedom to hear. The availability of the campus platform to outside speakers is a measure of the university's involvement with the issues of society as well as a measure of its commitment to freedom for its own students.

When members of a college were asked to examine the list of topics and to judge the freedom of speech given to students in the discussion of these issues, their problem was necessarily somewhat vague. What might "unpopular viewpoints" of students be? In what manner would they express them? To what extent would they attract public attention to their expression of these views? These questions were open to highly individual interpretation and a respondent's interpretation, no doubt, affected his estimate of the degree of permissiveness in his institution.

But the invitation of off-campus speakers presents more explicit situations for evaluation because the precise viewpoint and style of the specific speaker must be considered. An administrator, in examining a list of controversial speakers, is likely to be familiar with the record of these men in appearances at other institutions, and he remembers his experience with speakers in the past at his own college. Thus, for example, if he is asked whether or not he would allow Gus Hall to speak on campus he may be less apt to think of the educational value for students in hearing a Communist speak, or abstract freedom of speech, than of recent incidents at other schools, which remind him that any decision he makes will be highly unpopular with some segments of the local population.

It is for these reasons that the policies regarding off-campus speakers may be more indicative of the degree of freedom actually practiced in American institutions than are the answers to the free speech section of the questionnaire, considered in Chapter 3. When a university is confronted with the variety of complex considerations and pressures that off-campus speakers bring with them, do these considerations prevent the implementation of freedom in that institution? Are ideological preferences for free speech overshadowed by practical complexities? Just what reservations did administrators express when questioned about their speaker policy?

Their first point was that students should listen to all sides of an issue. This would mean, presumably, that if Martin Luther King were invited to speak, Governor Wallace or some spokesman for segregation should also be invited to provide a balance of opinion. This reflects an administrator's desire to assure that the college forum resemble classroom inquiry in allowing the student to examine many facets of a problem rather than only one. It seems appropriate to many college administrators that the thoughtful methods of academic inquiry be applied by both the speakers and the audiences using the college platform.

A second consideration arises from a desire of administrators to uphold the principles of fair play in the treatment of issues. Many speakers are controversial because they not only express unpopular viewpoints but also advocate unpopular actions. Should students be exposed to pleas for action? Those who say "no" would argue that men such as George Lincoln Rockwell have no place in the college environment because their pleas are visceral, not analytical, and their cunning emotional appeals for destructive action might prove dangerous to immature students. Some administrators seek to assure the educational value of the speaker by providing the student audience with the perspective of some preliminary knowledge of the man they are inviting.

A third consideration concerns the purpose of the students in inviting a guest to speak. As one president says, "I would want to know about the motives for the invitation. Do students want to ridicule? Look on social freaks? Seek entertainment or elucidation?" Or another, "Students want novelty. . . . They see novelty in extremes."

These three reservations seem to be consequences of the educator's conscious desire to envelop an off-campus speaker in an academic environment like that of classroom debate and discussion. Administrators are concerned lest the debate proceed without order, constructive intentions, or a careful examination of all sides of the issue. They are concerned that it may advance the propagation of a single viewpoint rather than the pursuit of truth. If they could be assured that a responsible atmosphere would prevail, they would assent. But because this is uncertain many of them do not hesitate to suppress any invitations which might involve demagoguery rather than scholarship.

Off-campus speakers present another kind of danger for the institution, closely linked with the danger of destroying the contemplative academic atmosphere. The university is under constant public scrutiny and, as one administrator laments, "People have not learned to distinguish between 'the college' and the people to whom it would allow a platform." This confusion between the college as a platform for controversial opinions and the college as an advocate of these opinions often takes place. Since it is not clear to the public that listening to radical viewpoints does not imply approval of them, but rather provides case studies for scholarly analysis, citizens' cries of protest sadly miss the point. One lady asked Chancellor Robert Hutchins of the University of Chicago whether it was a fact that communism was taught in his university. He replied, "Yes, madam, and we also teach cancer at our medical school."

If a student's freedom to hear any speaker contributes toward his own maturation as a learning exercise, is it relevant, therefore, to the mission of the institution? Are disturbances part of the price that is paid when educational goals are achieved? Does an open-speaker policy provide the students with an opportunity to apply the knowledge and reason acquired and developed in the classroom to the variety of issues available for debate, in the variety of ways an experienced and eloquent speaker can present them? Off-campus speakers are, for some, the raw material for academic analysis.

The Questionnaire

In the questionnaire were listed the names and identities of seventeen persons who had aroused controversy on some campuses where they had spoken. The list of speakers was drawn from a roster of more than fifty "controversial" campus speakers found in articles in the national weekly news magazines dating from October 1961 to November 1963.

The speakers listed in the questionnaire were as follows:

1. James R. Hoffa, president of the International Brotherhood of Teamsters
2. Robert N. Welch, founder of the John Birch Society
3. George C. Wallace, governor of Alabama

4. Robert P. Moses, field secretary of the Student Nonviolent Coordinating Committee
5. Barry Sheppard, national chairman of the Young Socialist Alliance
6. Malcolm X, New York leader of Black Muslims
7. Rev. Martin Luther King, Jr., head of the Southern Christian Leadership Conference
8. Barry Goldwater, U.S. senator from Arizona
9. Frank Wilkinson, chairman of the National Committee to Abolish the House Un-American Activities Committee
10. Brewster Kneen, youth secretary of Fellowship of Reconciliation
11. Augustin Cardinal Bea, head of the Vatican Secretariat for Promoting Christian Unity
12. Daniel Rubin, member and national youth director of the Communist Party
13. John P. Humphrey, director of the U.N. Human Rights Division
14. Earl Warren, chief justice of the U.S. Supreme Court
15. Oswald Mosley, founder of the British Fascist Movement
16. Fred Schwarz, president of the Christian Anti-Communism Crusade
17. George Lincoln Rockwell, head of the American Nazi Party

During the period that respondents had questionnaires (spring 1964) the status of each of the following was changing: James Hoffa was under indictment for jury tampering; George Wallace was speaking widely and engaged in several state primary contests for the Democratic presidential nomination; Malcolm X broke with the Black Muslims to establish the Black Nationalists (he was later assassinated, February 21, 1965, in New York City); Barry Goldwater was an active candidate for the Republican presidential nomination.

As a brief inspection of this speaker list will indicate, no single index of controversiality was used. The list includes persons representing many shades of opinion on a broad range of economic, political, social, and religious issues. The spectrum of speakers ranges from extreme left to extreme right, from reputability to notoriety—analysts and advocates.

Respondents were asked to indicate the following: (1) Which, if any, *have spoken* or *would be permitted* to speak on your campus? (2) Which, if any, might be considered so "controversial" that you think the administration would *strongly question the advisability* of their appearance?

The reader is cautioned not to assume that "advisability questioned" is synonymous with "cannot speak." On the free and open campus, questioning advisability might mean that the proposal to invite the speaker would be approved even though the wisdom of this approval was doubted. This interpretation was suggested from the fact that some respondents checked both "could speak" and "advisability questioned" on the list. At a slightly less permissive campus "advisability questioned" might indicate that a decision to permit or deny the invitation would be preceded by conferences between students and administrators, consultation with civic or political leaders, and consideration of serious outside pressures. At campuses where administrators judge that a speaker may not be directly relevant to educational goals, or could engender hostility within the campus or local community, or professes an ideology which is a radical departure from that of the institution, "advisability questioned" may be no more than a flat refusal to hear the speaker.

Although a "cannot speak" category, had it been used, would certainly have been less ambiguous than "advisability questioned," we assumed it would have been likely to discourage a negative reaction, particularly in the case of those administrators who hesitate to accept or condemn any speaker until they have examined the highly individual circumstances that accompany his invitation.

Because of these considerations the best indication of freedom on the campus is found in the response "could speak." Administrators responding "could speak" would accept the speaker, but those who did not were expressing some reluctance to grant permission for the invitation. Figures 10–12 present the speakers arranged in three groups, "acceptable," "controversial," and "highly controversial," according to responses of presidents and deans.

Acceptable Speakers

Dr. Hugo W. Thompson, chairman of a committee appointed to outline Macalester College's off-campus speaker policy, has said, "Speakers who have something original or significant to say in any realm are apt to be controversial."[4] This statement is substantiated by an examination of the responses to the first group of speakers. Each of the six most acceptable speakers—Earl Warren, Barry Goldwater, Martin Luther King, Jr., Augustin Cardinal Bea, Robert Moses, and John P. Humph-

[4] Hugo W. Thompson, "Open Platform at Macalester," *Macalester College Bulletin*, September 1963, p. 6.

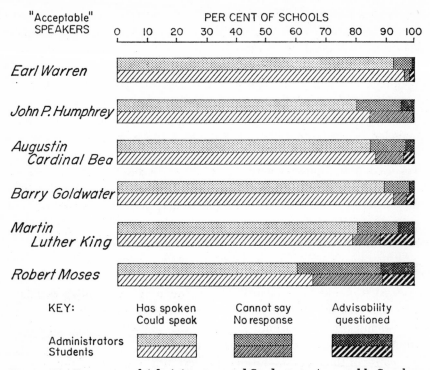

Figure 10. Responses of Administrators and Students to Acceptable Speakers

rey—would be unwelcome on some of our campuses. The most acceptable of these is Chief Justice Earl Warren (after whose name one president responded, "Are you kidding?"), yet 7 per cent of our campuses
would hesitate if students wished to invite him to speak. Two of the presidents participating in this study reported that their institutions had been
subjected to considerable criticism because he had been invited to or
had appeared on the campus. Eighteen presidents questioned the advisability of an invitation to Augustin Cardinal Bea, the man who is
credited with doing more than any other individual to advance the
worldwide Protestant-Catholic rapprochement in 1963 and 1964.[5]
Nineteen per cent of the deans and presidents responding would have
hesitated to permit the appearance of Negro leader Martin Luther King,
who, some months later, received the Nobel Prize for Peace. Small as

[5] Henry F. Van Dusen, "They Really Talked to Each Other," *New York Times
Book Review,* August 23, 1964, p. 6.

these percentages may be in contrast to the large percentage of administrators indicating that these men could speak, the finding is significant that even the most reputable of speakers may be refused the platform on some campuses.

Controversial Speakers

The seven controversial speakers are George C. Wallace, Frank Wilkinson, Fred Schwarz, Robert Welch, James Hoffa, Brewster Kneen, and Barry Sheppard. According to the administrators, they could speak or had spoken at 43 to 59 per cent of the responding institutions.

It is here that we find the highest proportion of administrators checking "cannot say." This may be explained in part by the relative ob-

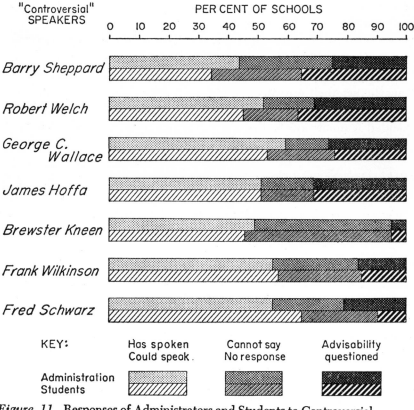

Figure 11. Responses of Administrators and Students to Controversial Speakers

scurity of some of the names in this group. Brewster Kneen, for example, is not well known in American public life. His Fellowship of Reconciliation is a religious pacifist group of 13,000 members operating predominantly among Protestant Christians and numbering 300 local groups. For the administrators and students not responding to Kneen, the name "Fellowship of Reconciliation" may have had little meaning. On the other hand, the name of Frank Wilkinson may have been unfamiliar to many, but his title, "chairman of the National Committee to Abolish the House Un-American Activities Committee," clearly identifies him. Likewise, "president of the Christian Anti-Communism Crusade" provides a fairly clear identification of Fred Schwarz. Yet relatively few respondents were able to evaluate the advisability of permitting these speakers on their campuses; they would neither question the advisability of inviting these speakers nor say they could appear. Either the respondents needed more identification than was provided in a brief description or they wanted to know the specific conditions under which the speaker would be invited. In which direction would the decision of these respondents be made if they had to make a choice? It is not certain whether their answers would have been permissive or restrictive, but an analysis of the response patterns indicated that those who responded "cannot say" tended more frequently to question advisability when they did respond.

Highly Controversial Speakers

Four of the speakers, the presidents and deans said, would be welcomed at fewer than one-third of the nation's campuses: George Lincoln Rockwell, Sir Oswald Mosley, Daniel Rubin, and Malcolm X (see Figure 12). These speakers have advocated solutions to major political and social issues which, if accepted, would tend to destroy the very freedom which permits them to advance their views. Their positions may be unacceptable to the academic community, yet it is in this way that these men test our ability to tolerate and analyze even that which we may ultimately reject and oppose.

The administrators in our study must have recognized that an invitation to any one of these speakers would almost certainly result in controversy on the campus. The one-third of them or less who indicated that these men could speak on their campuses did so in the awareness that they might have to pay a high price for their decisions.

70

INVITATION OF CONTROVERSIAL SPEAKERS

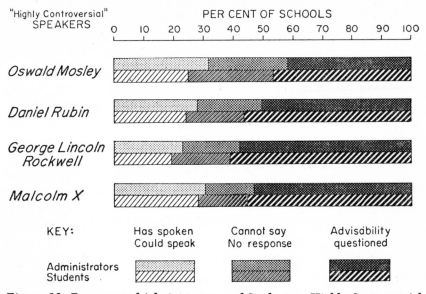

Figure 12. Responses of Administrators and Students to Highly Controversial Speakers

George Lincoln Rockwell, leader of the American Nazi Party, is the least acceptable of the seventeen speakers on the list, according to all respondents. He would have been permitted to speak at only 23 per cent of the campuses. A number of administrators said that although he would be permitted to speak they questioned the advisability of having him on their campuses, suggesting that their policies will permit any speaker, but that what Rockwell would say or do is anathema to them.

The other three highly controversial speakers were only slightly more acceptable. Malcolm X and Oswald Mosley would have been permitted at a third of the schools and Daniel Rubin at 28 per cent. More than half of the institutions queried would question the advisability of three of these four speakers.

Attitudes regarding off-campus speakers differ widely depending on the nature of the institution and its geographical location. Which kinds of institutions, first of all, would permit all seventeen speakers? Table 10 lists the percentage of presidents at each type of institution responding "could speak" to all seventeen names. The highest response comes from large public universities and nonsectarian universities; at 41 per cent of these schools presidents indicated that all listed speakers would be permitted. Catholic colleges and universities rank lowest—only 1 per cent of the Catholic liberal arts college presidents would permit all seventeen speakers and none of the Catholic university presidents would do so. Teachers' colleges and Protestant liberal arts colleges are apparently very selective in their choice of speakers. Only 12 per cent of the teachers' colleges would permit all seventeen as would only 7 per cent of the Protestant liberal arts colleges.

Table 10. Percentage of Schools, by Institutional Category, Reporting All Listed
Speakers Had Spoken or Would Be Permitted to Speak
(According to Presidents)

Institutional Category	All Listed Speakers Would Be Permitted to Speak	None of Listed Speakers Had Spoken since Fall 1961
Universities		
Large public..........	41**	25**
Small public	22*	67
Private	41**	36**
Protestant	26*	44**
Catholic	0**	75
Colleges		
Private	31**	57**
Protestant	7**	73*
Catholic	1**	95**
Teachers'	12**	84**
Technical	19	75
All categories	17	69

* This percentage is significantly different from the percentage for all categories at the .05 level.
** This percentage is significantly different from the percentage for all categories at the .01 level.

Thus, few of the institutions would permit all seventeen speakers—fewer than half of even the most permissive types of institutions. The inclusion of four or five speakers on our list who have caused violent reactions in many college communities where they have appeared permitted our question to measure an aspect of the exercise of student academic freedom that most institutions do not encourage. In this way, it was possible to distinguish the practitioners from the preachers of unqualified academic freedom for students. If an institution is theoretically committed without qualification to the exercise of student freedom then one might expect that it would accept all seventeen speakers. Few institutions, indeed, meet this standard.

72

Where Have They Spoken?

One would expect to find that the listed speakers have spoken more often on campuses where speakers, in general, would be permitted to speak, but there are exceptions. As Table 10 shows, certain kinds of institutions whose climate is not unfavorable to off-campus speakers—the technical schools, for example—have not, in fact, had these speakers on their campuses very frequently. In 75 per cent of the technical institutions none of the seventeen speakers had appeared. Perhaps the student body is too specialized to show much interest in societal issues discussed by the speakers on the list. That none of these men has appeared at 67 per cent of the small universities suggests that these schools, while not unusually antipathetic to off-campus speakers, may simply be too small and too obscure to attract men of national reputation. Although considerations such as these explain disparities between "has spoken" and "could speak" responses, the general trends are the same. Most listed speakers had appeared, if at all, in public and private nonsectarian schools where they are most frequently considered welcome. They are least acceptable to, and have appeared least often at, the Catholic schools and the teachers' colleges.

The highly controversial speaker is a most rigorous test of academic

Table 11. Percentage of Respondents, by Institutional Category, Reporting Highly Controversial Speakers Had Spoken or Would Be Permitted to Speak

Institutional Category	Oswald Mosley	Daniel Rubin	Malcolm X	George Rockwell
Universities				
Large public	54**	50**	56**	49**
Small public	38**	33**	35	32**
Private	60**	60**	69**	41**
Protestant	20*	22	28	22
Catholic	12**	12**	12**	6**
Colleges				
Private	46**	42**	46**	34**
Protestant	22**	19**	20**	14**
Catholic	8**	6**	10**	4**
Teachers'	21**	18**	22**	15**
Technical	29	24	32	20
All categories	28	26	30	21

* This percentage is significantly different from the percentage for all categories at the .05 level.
** This percentage is significantly different from the percentage for all categories at the .01 level.

73

freedom. Which institutions were most willing to let students hear Oswald Mosley, George Lincoln Rockwell, Daniel Rubin, and the late Malcolm X, all of whom have been known to create a painful complex of problems for institutions? Table 11 indicates the degree to which each type of institution was significantly above or below the average for all types of institutions. The dichotomy between nonsectarian and sectarian schools reveals itself here with greater clarity than in the preceding examinations of data. Public and private nonsectarian universities and liberal arts colleges are significantly more permissive than average in their willingness to permit students to listen to these four most controversial figures, whereas both Protestant and Catholic liberal arts colleges reveal considerably less permissiveness than average. Protestant universities, however, are far from being as restrictive in this respect as Catholic universities, which respond in a manner very similar to that of the Catholic colleges.

Teachers' colleges fall significantly below the mean in their willingness to invite these speakers, a similar tendency to that observed earlier in the analysis of freedom of topic discussion; here the trend is even stronger. Although teachers' colleges did not distinguish themselves by

Table 12. Percentage of Respondents, by Institutional Category, Reporting Controversial Speakers Had Spoken or Would Be Permitted to Speak

Institutional Category	Barry Sheppard	Robert Welch	George Wallace	James Hoffa	Brewster Kneen	Frank Wilkinson	Fred Schwarz
Universities							
Large public.	68**	78**	88**	77**	66**	82**	80**
Small public.	50**	65**	73**	66**	49	64**	66*
Private	76**	80**	77**	78**	76**	87**	80**
Protestant ..	28**	45	62	43	41	50	61
Catholic	20**	38*	30**	44	19**	44**	46**
Colleges							
Private	58**	64**	71**	62**	62**	68**	73**
Protestant ...	32	42**	56	45**	50**	52	58
Catholic	12**	20**	19**	25**	14**	36**	44**
Teachers' ...	31**	38**	54	48	35**	46**	50**
Technical	32	48	56	58	41	56	50
All categories..	38	48	55	51	44	56	59

* This percentage is significantly different from the percentage for all categories at the .05 level.

** This percentage is significantly different from the percentage for all categories at the .01 level.

any unusual rigidity or restrictiveness in educational philosophy, student freedoms seem severely limited in practice.

These same generalizations apply to the larger group of speakers of average controversiality, as shown in Table 12. Those schools whose response to highly controversial speakers was far more restrictive than average are also significantly more restrictive when the speakers are somewhat less controversial. This implies that for these institutions the degree of controversiality is not the major consideration. If *any* controversy is likely the speaker is likely to be considered unwelcome.

It is not until the schools are compared in their responses to acceptable speakers (see Table 13) that some distinctions become apparent among those institutions which rank highly permissive with regard to

Table 13. Percentage of Respondents, by Institutional Category, Reporting Acceptable Speakers Had Spoken or Would Be Permitted to Speak

Institutional Category	Earl Warren	Barry Goldwater	Augustin Cardinal Bea	John P. Humphrey	Martin Luther King	Robert Moses
Universities						
Large public ..	96	96*	90	90**	85	81**
Small public ..	91*	93	84	81	79	66
Private	95	96*	93**	94**	92**	87**
Protestant	97	95	78*	72**	77	48**
Catholic	95	90	98**	78	85	61
Colleges						
Private	95	94	87	89**	84*	76**
Protestant	93	94	79**	82	76*	64
Catholic	96*	90	97**	84	83	51**
Teachers'	92	86**	77**	73**	69**	54**
Technical	90	89	78*	78	74	57
All categories ...	94	92	86	82	80	64

* This percentage is significantly different from the percentage for all categories at the .05 level.
** This percentage is significantly different from the percentage for all categories at the .01 level.

controversial speakers. While large public universities and private nonsectarian universities continue to rank much higher than average—even when the average, in the case of acceptable speakers, is very high—the small public universities and, to a lesser extent, the private liberal arts colleges, fall much nearer the mean. This indicates that their permissiveness, while impressive, does not match the record established by the large public universities and nonsectarian universities. The type of school most reluctant to accept these men as speakers are the teachers' colleges, which again are significantly below average.

The over-all pattern of response to our list of seventeen speakers cannot be described as generally permissive. The least acceptable group of persons would be permitted on no more than a third of our campuses and the most acceptable at no more than 94 per cent. Ranking highest above the average in permissiveness are private universities, then the large and small public universities and private liberal arts colleges. At or near the mean are technical institutions and Protestant universities, and least permissive of all are the teachers' colleges, the Catholic universities, and finally Catholic liberal arts colleges.

Table 14. Percentage of Respondents, by Geographical Region, Reporting Speakers Had Spoken or Would Be Permitted to Speak

Speakers	New England	Middle Atlantic	North Central	North Western	Southern	Western	All Regions
Highly controversial							
Oswald Mosley	43**	35**	28	32	14**	35	28
Daniel Rubin	44**	31**	24	25	12**	32	26
George Lincoln Rockwell	31**	24	20	27*	11**	30*	21
Malcolm X	54**	38**	26**	29	14**	46**	30
Controversial							
Barry Sheppard	53**	46**	38	38	21**	52**	38
Robert Welch	60**	54**	46	60**	33**	60**	48
George Wallace	64**	55	55	64*	50*	61	55
James Hoffa	66**	52	52	57	38**	60*	51
Brewster Kneen	54**	49*	44	44	35**	51	44
Frank Wilkinson	66**	61*	55	53	45**	67**	56
Fred Schwarz	62	62	59	64	49**	78**	59
Robert Moses	74**	74**	65	64	45**	72*	64
Acceptable							
Earl Warren	95	96	95	98*	88**	97	94
Augustin Cardinal Bea	90	90**	87	80*	76**	94**	86
Barry Goldwater	92	93	93	98**	86**	94	92
Martin Luther King	91**	87**	84**	90**	55**	76	80
John P. Humphrey	85	89**	85**	78	72**	82	82

* This percentage is significantly different from the percentage for all regions at the .05 level.

** This percentage is significantly different from the percentage for all regions at the .01 level.

Geographical Distribution

The geographical distribution of the responding institutions (see Table 14) indicates there is significantly less permissiveness for *all* types of speakers in the South, and considerably greater than average freedom for students to invite controversial speakers in the New England and middle Atlantic states. The West ranks next in openness. Additional analysis revealed that the greatest variation appeared among public universities, which rank very low in the South and very high in the West. Catholic schools, regardless of geographical location, rank low.

Congruity of Perception

Because administrators generally determine policy, our analysis has centered on their responses to off-campus speakers as a direct indication of the existence of the freedom for students to hear speakers. The amount of agreement between deans and presidents is remarkable. So is the similarity we found in the answers of the two student respondents. Larger differences can be observed between students and administrators, although they are generally in agreement. When asked to estimate the degree of permissiveness at their schools toward acceptable speakers, students showed a slight, but insignificant, tendency to view their campuses as freer than did administrators. But in the case of controversial speakers the reverse tendency was observed. Students expected more restriction than administrators said they would exercise—and in the case of the four most controversial figures, this tendency for students to perceive greater restriction was even more marked. Catholic schools are a consistent exception to this. In Catholic institutions students tend to view their campuses as more open than do administrators, even in the case of the most controversial speakers.

A tentative explanation for the tendency of students to perceive less freedom than administrators do in almost every case is that students, in their drive to gain more freedom, probably like to represent themselves as having less freedom than they actually have. Conversely, administrators wishing to restrain this drive for increased freedom may like to view themselves as being permissive. This assumption would seem to apply except for acceptable speakers, where students expect administrators to be more permissive than they claim they would be. This may be explained by the supposition that students are more easily impressed by these nationwide figures than are more mature and experienced administrators. Students might think that administrators would not dare to turn these men down. In Catholic universities students' respect for authority may be even higher and so this effect extends to all speakers rather than simply the most reputable groups as at the other schools.

Off-Campus Speaker Policy

How is it decided whether a man will be permitted to speak? How much criticism results, and from what sources? Is the existence of a written policy on speakers related to the degree of freedom accorded students in inviting speakers? These questions were investigated in our questionnaire in an attempt to illuminate the procedures and pressures connected with speaker situations.

Presidents and deans were first asked, "Does your institution have a *written policy* dealing with the invitation of off-campus speakers by student organizations?" Sixty-five per cent of respondents said "no." Those who indicated that no written policy existed were also asked if traditions or precedents served as guidelines instead, and fewer than half said "yes." Thus, although most schools are apparently governed by written policy or traditional guidelines, one-third of all respondents indicated that no clear precedents existed for decision-making.

What guidelines remain for the schools where no directives exist? Decisions are apparently highly idiosyncratic, are not likely to follow formal procedural lines, and probably result more from immediate pressures than from the wish to implement a university philosophy of student freedom. Decisions are apt to reflect the temperament of the man who makes them and the bases for these decisions may fluctuate—from day to day, from year to year, and, of course, from speaker to speaker.

What kinds of institutions have written policy? Are freer and bolder decisions made when the university can judge each case on its own merits without being hampered by too many specific criteria? Or does the existence of written policy ensure that a liberal institutional philosophy is actually applied to each invitation? Responses to our questionnaire indicate that the same institutions whose speaker policy is permissive are generally those who put that policy in writing. The correlation between written policy and a permissive environment is high, but it is not clear whether the existence of written policy is the cause or the effect of a permissive atmosphere at the school. Possession of written policy may encourage the application of liberal principles to actual practice.

78

Or permissive schools may simply prefer written policy in order to publicize their socially approved principles. Perhaps by the time an institution has grown large and diversified enough to codify policy, the process of growth itself has encouraged the formulation of a liberal policy.

Presidents and deans were asked, "During the past two and one-half years have proposed invitations, actual invitations, or the appearance of off-campus speakers brought about considerable criticism from sources inside or outside the campus?" Thirty-two per cent answered "yes," indicating that much public attention is attracted to university visitors and that, at least a third of the time, it takes a critical form. If at a third of our campuses "considerable" criticism has been aroused, one may infer that there has been some lesser degree of ill-feeling from time to time at many others.

The preceding discussion has dealt with responses to a list of seventeen persons who have spoken on some American college or university campuses. No claim has been made that the list of speakers represents all, or even most, of the many views on the many societal problems needing solution. In another part of the questionnaire presidents were asked to identify speakers whose invitation or appearance had caused considerable criticism since the fall of 1961. More than two hundred individuals were named. One was mentioned by twenty-three presidents—Gus Hall —but most were mentioned only once.

The list of names included, along with an expected assortment of Communists, Socialists, Birchites, segregationists and integrationists, such persons as the late President John F. Kennedy, President Lyndon B. Johnson, John Ciardi (poetry editor of the *Saturday Review*), and Linus Pauling. The list, reproduced in part on page 80, is convincing evidence that there are probably only a few persons whose appearance as a guest speaker would not cause controversy on some campus in the United States. When asked to identify major sources of criticism from inside or outside the campus, administrators pointed to off-campus conservative groups, especially the John Birch Society, as their severest critics. Other community disapproval came frequently from citizens at large (especially alumni or parents of students who made their views known through the local press or broadcasting stations), from members of the local clergy, and less frequently from legislators and ethnic minority groups. Criticism from within the campus arose almost as often,

NAMES OF SPEAKERS SUBMITTED AS CONTROVERSIAL BY ONE OR MORE PRESIDENTS

Names Submitted by More Than Two Presidents, with Number of Submissions in Parentheses

Gus Hall (23)
Martin Luther King, Jr. (13)
Governor George Wallace (12)
George Lincoln Rockwell (13)
Frank Wilkinson (10)
Malcolm X (9)
Barry Goldwater (8)

Norman Thomas (8)
Governor Ross Barnett (7)
Dr. Herbert Aptheker (7)
Daniel Rubin (5)
Dorothy Healy (5)
Madame Ngo Dinh Nhu (5)
Ben Davis (5)
William Worthy (4)

James Meredith (4)
William Buckley (4)
Mulford Q. Sibley (3)
William Douglas (3)
John Cogley (3)
Roy Wilkins (3)
Pete Seeger (3)
Fulton Lewis III (3)
Gordon Hall (3)
Linus Pauling (3)

Names Submitted by Two Presidents

Eleanor Roosevelt
Paul Douglas
Dick Gregory
J. Strom Thurmond
Walter Judd
Gov. Nelson Rockefeller
James Farmer
Russell Kirk

Scott Nearing
Langston Hughes
Barry Sheppard
Justice Earl Warren
William Mandel
John Rousselot
James Baldwin
Louis Lomax

Father Hans Kung
Dorothy Day
Dr. Ralph Bunche
Drew Pearson
James Lawson
Herman Lumer
Dr. L. P. Weaver
Norman Cousins

Names Submitted by One President

Elizabeth Flynn
Max Lerner
Billy Graham
Mike Monroney
G. Colin Jackson
Michael Scriven
Mike Mansfield
Carl Winter
Josh White
Harold Urey
Eunice Shriver
Rev. Milan Opocensky

Edward Kennedy
John Kenneth Galbraith
Clement Atlee
Philip Scharper
Tom Duggan
Laurence Ferlinghetti
Oswald Mosley
Paul Sweezy
Dr. Walter Strokes
Felix Greene
Rev. Malcolm Boyd
Milton Rosen
Harry T. Everingham

Raya Dunayevskoya
Sol Mendelson
Edward Annis
Geryl Rubiens
Charles Malik
Harlow Shapely
Lin Yutang
Lillian Hellman
Thurgood Marshall
Robert Williams
Adam Clayton Powell
W. D. Snodgrass

coming from students and faculty generally rather than from organized campus groups.

Certain community groups appear to consider it their duty to police campus speaker invitations, judging from the frequency with which the D.A.R., the American Legion, and the John Birch Society are mentioned. Although these conservative groups, singled out by many administrators as major sources of criticism, attempt to discourage the expression of viewpoints opposed to their own, leftist organizations were less frequently cited as sources of criticism. Evidently the right-wing critics are less tolerant of opposing views than organizations at the other end of the political spectrum, or perhaps left-wing speakers are more often invited by student groups to speak on the campus. In any case, the disproportionate amount of criticism coming from conservative organizations indicates that they are a vocal and critical element in many academic communities.

The conviction among some citizens that radicals should be denied the university forum is mirrored in the creation of an Emergency Committee to Halt the Spread of Nazism in American Colleges and Universities, a group dedicated to silencing George Lincoln Rockwell. In the statement of the purpose of the organization we read:

College and university students are simply too ill-informed and immature to be allowed to judge Rockwell themselves. He is too slick for them and too pat—too devilishly clever to permit students to expose themselves to him. To allow college and university students to hear Rockwell is NOT "free speech." It is exactly like letting babies sample poisoned candy. They don't know enough—they haven't experienced enough—to judge for themselves whether they should even try a sample . . . the average college student, while he feels himself well-informed and mature in judgment is actually a born sucker for the kind of slick facts and "Alice in Wonderland" arguments of demagogues like Rockwell.[6]

This quotation gives a good indication of the depth of feeling that inspires the antipathy of some community groups, and their consequent persistence. A college administrator who wishes to implement a liberal interpretation of freedom of speech at his campus invites the antagonism of these groups whose outcries can, if the community at large is receptive, do much to limit his freedom in decision-making.

The two student respondents more frequently reported criticism of speaker policy than did their administrators. Whereas 32 per cent of administrators reported some pressure, 37 per cent of the students did so. Two possible reasons for this difference suggest themselves. The student respondent's field of perception only partially overlaps that of the administrator's. Students are perhaps aware of many kinds of criticism expressed informally and *sotto voce,* during discussions carried on among students in college fraternities and clubs, for example. And both student respondents, because their official positions might enable them to pro-

---

[6] John Carlson and Jacob Cohen, *Emergency Committee to Halt the Spread of Nazism in American Colleges and Universities* (Cambridge, Mass., n.d.; mimeographed, 3 pp.)

mote some kind of action, undoubtedly hear much criticism from those who hope they will channel it to higher authority. It may be, too, that students are simply more sensitive to criticism of their institution because they do not have the toughened skins of administrators, who may be inclined to minimize rather than maximize wounds.

The Decision-Making Process

It is up to the dean of students in most institutions to decide whether, and on what basis, permission will be granted for the appearance of a speaker who has a reputation for stirring up controversy. Whom does he consult? Respondents were asked, "When considering whether to grant permission for the appearance of a specific controversial speaker, which of the following sources of information or opinion are you most likely to consult?" In 83 per cent of the institutions the dean is most likely to consult the president. Forty-three per cent of the deans indicated that they would consult the student group inviting the speaker—a surprisingly small percentage, unless it is assumed that the remainder consulted the student group at the time the invitation was offered. Thirty-five per cent of deans would consult other administrators, and 30 per cent would consult the student body president. The proportion of deans indicating that they would confer with the student body president suggests that at many colleges the judgment of this student officer is highly valued, or perhaps he is brought in only to provide further information on the nature of the speaker and the reasons for the invitation, or to gain student support for the dean's decision. Most of the deans checked more than one source of information or opinion, indicating that in critical situations many arguments are heard before a final decision is announced.

Presidents were asked, "Since the fall of 1961 have situations involving proposed or actual invitation of off-campus speakers become critical enough to be brought to your attention for prior review?" Thirty-one per cent answered "yes." Those who answered "yes" were asked a series of questions to determine how a final decision was reached. First they were asked which sources of information or opinion were particularly helpful. Many sources were checked, the most frequent being the dean of students, other administrators, and the student body president. It becomes apparent that in decisions regarding off-campus speakers the student body president ranks high among the persons both the deans and presidents consult. Few presidents reported that consultation with community leaders, alumni, or donors was especially helpful, and only 11 per cent of the presidents found consultation with their governing boards helpful.

Public Clarification of Policy

The opinion of the American Civil Liberties Union stated earlier suggests that public clarification of a university's speaker policy—asserting that the university does not necessarily subscribe to views expressed by its guest speakers—may be one means of preventing damage to university public relations without curbing the freedom of students to invite whom they please. How frequently do institutions interpret their speaker policy to the public and under what circumstances? When a controversial speaker was permitted, and when he also occasioned a storm of protest from the public, then 44 per cent of the presidents issued public statements. If, however, he spoke without incident, only 26 per cent issued public statements, evidently feeling that it was better not to stir up the waters.

The attention a speaker is apt to attract is a major consideration for the determination of policy in some institutions. One president commenting on the speaker policy of his institution said that he would be far more likely to allow the invitation if the speaker was the private guest of a student organization, but that he would hesitate before granting a hearing to a speech publicized as a university-wide event.

Presidents who had not been faced with important decisions on controversial speakers were asked much the same question. Did they, too, publicly interpret the educational philosophy of their institutions? Only 22 per cent said "yes." Although most universities thus have not publicly stated their policy, those that have permitted an invitation which embroiled them in controversy have frequently clarified their policy.

Diversity prevails in speaker policy. This fact alone might explain the existence of considerable confusion and disagreement about the university's role in the acceptance of controversial off-campus speakers. As we have seen, written policy is in effect at a minority of our institutions and at one-third of them no clear guidelines for decision-making exist. Although a high correlation was found between the presence of written policy and permissiveness in inviting speakers, it is by no means clear that the formulation of written policy makes the administrator's task easier, since our findings show that those permissive institutions which allow more controversial speakers also receive more criticism. Pugnacious community organizations interfere with the institution's freedom to determine its own policy and some are expressly dedicated to curbing freedom of students to hear whom they please. It is no wonder that universities are not uniform in issuing public policy statements; many are not eager to attract the spotlight.

It is encouraging that such a high proportion of institutions indicate that consultation is an essential part of any decision regarding a controversial speaker. Deans and presidents appear to be working closely together in the determination of speaker policy, and other administrators and the student body presidents are called in for advice. It may well be that if it becomes easier to make these decisions in the future, if speaker decisions become routine, this will have been achieved through consultation to find acceptable policy guidelines. Our data neither support nor reject this obiter dictum, however.

Summary

Questions concerning the invitation of speakers call to mind more explicit situations than do questions regarding free discussion, and hence provide a more objective measure of freedom as it is actually exercised. Since an outsider is being admitted to the groves of academe, attitudes toward speaker invitations also reflect the institution's involvement with the community. Speakers may not be directly relevant to the educational purpose of the university: frequently they expound a single, biased viewpoint; they are sometimes demagogues rather than scholars; and the motivation of the students in extending an invitation may not be academic. Further, powerful elements of the outside community sometimes exert pressures on the university to refuse a platform to certain men. Although many administrators reported their students had sufficient maturity and analytical skill to make good use of the opportunity to hear speakers, the factors just mentioned may explain the finding that there is considerably less freedom for students to hear controversial speakers than for student organizations to take unpopular stands on socially divisive issues. The acceptability of speakers varies widely, both from speaker to speaker and from school to school, but not even the most reputable of men can be heard in some schools.

The greatest freedom to hear speakers is found, in order of the most to the least permissive, at private universities, large and small public universities, and private liberal arts colleges. Protestant universities and technical institutions fall at the mean. Less than average freedom is found at the Protestant liberal arts colleges, the Catholic universities and liberal arts colleges, and the least is found at teachers' colleges.

There is more than average permissiveness with regard to this form of student freedom in the New England and middle Atlantic states and less in the South.

Written policy is in effect at one-third of the schools and these are the more permissive. Strong criticism is felt in about one-third of the schools, mainly from conservative organizations. The students perceived more criticism than did administrators. The dean frequently consults the president, other administrators, and the student body president in reaching decisions concerning off-campus speakers. The institution's policy is often publicly clarified when a speaker incites controversy and criticism, but a public statement of policy is not otherwise typical.

Students perceive less freedom in this area than do administrators, except as regards the most reputable speakers, and except for students at Catholic institutions, who perceive more freedom than administrators.

We turn now to an aspect of student freedom which tests institutions even more: the direct involvement of students in the community.

5 ⚡

Freedom of Organized Protest Action

IF student organizations discuss divisive social issues or invite speakers to discuss them they are likely to decide that action is needed to ameliorate some social ill. How can they then press for the implementation of that action? They can petition, campaign, picket, "sit-in," or express themselves in some other demonstrative way. Or can they? What limitations do colleges impose on this sort of activity?

Earlier it was suggested that student action may not be as clearly defensible a part of academic freedom as is student freedom of thought and expression. The intellectual is traditionally a man of contemplative wisdom rather than incisive action. As students become involved in action to improve society they may lose the perspective needed for a true understanding of the very problems they are trying to solve. This is a dilemma which faces any activist but should it be faced by the student? Learning is his primary job, according to some who would say that it is not too much to ask that he spend four years in the "ivory tower" carefully considering society's problems before he tries to implement his "right" answer. Thus it is contended that the university is a setting appropriate to the techniques of thoughtful seminar analysis, not threats of mob action.

With the increased incidence of retraining and going back to school, for persons at all levels of age and position, the "ivory tower" is becoming less removed from society. No more does one "learn" for four years

86

in college and then "do" for the rest of his life. Perhaps in our specialized and technical society even one's formal education may not ever formally come to an end.

Today's curriculum, with its emphasis on contemporary social issues, bears little resemblance to the classical education of colonial days when the study of Greek and Latin was thought to instill order in unruly minds. Today we educate future citizens by encouraging them to debate and analyze in the classroom the issues which they will someday face. The procedure is similar to the clinical technique in the training of physicians, or the case study approach in training lawyers. In modern education the emphasis is on the present *and* the future, pointing toward the time when the student becomes a productive member of society. It is thus not difficult to perceive why students are inclined not only to discuss but also to act on these same issues.

Student-initiated action in the extracurriculum is of great potential value as a pedagogical technique. The student is first of all acting with greater independence than he could in the classroom. Even the lack of experienced supervision has some value: mistakes also teach and their lessons are often less easily forgotten than those learned from books or teachers. Then too he is held responsible for the consequences of his actions, whereas in the classroom he may advance ideas without awareness of their ultimate consequences. Furthermore, students participating in activities out of class are testing ideas they have arrived at through study and critical examination. As they act out their allegiance to hypotheses and enlist the support of others, the failure or success of these ideas will be of real concern to them. Lessons learned in this highly charged atmosphere are likely to be remembered.

Moreover, students learn that changing society is not easy—that the complexity of any problem is almost infinite and that progress and change are often slow. This discovery should demonstrate the usefulness of careful academic analysis before action is initiated. Also, by involving themselves in contemporary social problems students develop a compassion for humanity. This sympathy for the unfortunate and the desire to improve their lot will, it is to be hoped, endure through the student's life, and may in itself better our society. Broad lessons such as these are offered by the extracurriculum. Ideas which have survived classroom discussion and debate have their most rigorous test in the battlefield of action.

Even though freedom of students' action may be educationally desirable it nevertheless presents very real dangers for the college. Students may be involved in violence—either giving or receiving it—and they may be arrested for civil or criminal offenses. Executives in business or government may indeed strongly disapprove of the students' activities and as a result withdraw their financial support from the college unless these activities are checked. Finally, aroused feelings of violence may exacerbate rather than illuminate scholarly inquiry and interfere with the institution's mission of attempting to understand societal problems.

Thus, there are theoretical arguments both for and against permitting students to act on social issues in their status as students as contrasted with their status as citizens. Whatever the theory, the fact is that some students desire the freedom to participate in such activity. In the words of Mario Savio, uttered, just before his arrest in 1964, at a student "free speech" demonstration at Sproul Hall on the Berkeley campus of the University of California:

The university is the place where people begin seriously to question the conditions of their existence and raise the issue whether they can be committed to the society they have been born into. After a long period of apathy during the 50's, students have begun not only to question but, having arrived at answers, to act on these answers . . . This free speech fight points up a fascinating aspect of contemporary campus life. Students are permitted to talk all they want so long as their speech has no consequences.[1]

It is quite clear that Savio's "free speech" movement was not really aiming at free speech—on the Berkeley campus, as elsewhere in the country, students already enjoyed much freedom of inquiry. The incident which precipitated the demonstrations and typified the chief issue at stake—if indeed most of the demonstrators had a clear notion of what issue was at stake—involved the freedom of students to organize and solicit other students for off-campus sociopolitical activity, in some cases illegal trespassing.

It is ironical but not inexplicable that student demonstrations demanding the freedom for greater involvement with the community should take place at Berkeley. None other than Clark Kerr, president of the

[1] Mario Savio, "An End to History," *Humanity*, December 1964. Cited by Michael V. Miller and Susan Gilmore, eds., *Revolution at Berkeley* (New York: Dell, 1965), p. 241.

University of California, is the originator of the concept "multiversity." He holds that the university should be *in* and *of* the world, training skilled intellects to perform useful functions in society, suiting its curriculum to the needs of the community. President Kerr does not expect his students to remain aloof from the problems of their society, and, as indicated above, students at Berkeley enjoy much freedom. Yet although this is true, Berkeley students were limited in their freedom of action and expression concerning political issues.

Granting that the methods of his movement may have been deplorable, Savio made a cogent objection to the multiversity. As the size of the university grows and as its involvement with society increases, the university may become committed to conserving the status quo, perhaps good and bad together. The university may lose its visionary role in society and students may be trained to serve in society, rather than encouraged to question and to improve it. Savio argues that students and professors alike should be free to experiment with methods of social transformation and to explore new ideas, without the restrictions of conservative convention. Freedom for the university to transform society as well as to conserve and transmit its accumulated knowledge is essential. Clark Kerr does not disparage this goal, but he thinks the multiversity can fulfill both functions. Savio, and the students who supported him, seemed to contend that it was failing to permit the students to work for those social changes in which they believed.

It was established in Chapter 3 that students can "talk all they want," as Savio said, but can they act on their convictions? Only by asking college students and administrators the extent to which certain types of demonstrative activity would be permitted could we determine how far administrators might be willing to carry the principle of academic freedom for students. Would they allow implementation of that principle when it involves lawful picketing and demonstration, alienation of certain community groups, or civil disobedience? What would be their attitude toward action on an issue whose relevance to the educational aim of the institution is debatable?

In answering the questionnaire one dean flatly stated, "Our students are restricted in social and political matters if *action* is involved." Another said, "Sure we believe in personal and academic freedom; we encourage our students to be responsible and mature individuals. Approximately 85 per cent of our students participated in . . . demonstrations in the local community." How many and what kinds of colleges are at these extremes, and which are in the middle?

The Questionnaire

Respondents were presented with a list of nine situations—nine forms of action which students might take:

1. Student organization pickets a public meeting.
2. Student organization sits in at a local lunch counter.
3. Student government publishes a resolution speaking for student body without a prior referendum.
4. Student government publishes a resolution speaking for student body with a prior referendum.
5. Students organize a group to advocate an extreme position on a controversial issue.
6. Student organization sends a petition to a government agency or officials.
7. Student organization invites a controversial off-campus speaker.
8. Student political organization campaigns on the campus for the election of a candidate in a national election.
9. Student editor writes an editorial expressing extreme viewpoints on a controversial issue.

All the items may require administrative decision as to the permissibility of these procedural, rather than substantive, matters. That is, is picketing of a meeting or campaigning on the campus for a national political candidate a procedure proper for students to undertake? The questionnaire did not provide clarifying details, such as the signs the pickets might be carrying, the platform or manners of the political candidate, or the wording on campaign literature. No doubt the attitude of the administration would vary considerably, depending on whether the students were at a Mafia meeting carrying signs reading "we protest lawlessness," or picketing a meeting of an ecumenical council with obscenities printed on their placards. The group to be picketed, the words to be printed on signs, and the anticipated disruption of order would have a bearing on the permissiveness of the administration, but respondents were asked simply to indicate whether picketing per se, or any of the other listed situations, represented a legitimate student activity toward which the administration would be permissive.

The answers of the respondents no doubt reflected their own personal experiences with the possible ends to which these techniques could be used, the motivations of the students employing them, and the outraged reactions of community groups. Eliciting such associations was, however, our object. Rather than specify each of these variables in asking the questions, we preferred to let each respondent draw on his own past experiences because these would condition his future conduct, whether he be a student deciding whether or how to use a demonstrative technique, or an administrator deciding whether to permit its use. Hence, the answers to these questions provide a close approximation of the permissiveness of college administrators toward demonstrative techniques.

Respondents were given the following instruction: "Keeping in mind the complexity of each situation, please estimate the 'permissiveness' of your college on each of the following situations." Degrees of response offered were "quite permissive," "fairly permissive," "not permissive," or "cannot say." As explained earlier, the word "permissive" was used to avoid discouraging negative reactions and to reflect accurately the terms of administrators' thought and action.

The Responses

Figure 13 presents the responses of students and administrators to the nine situations listed in the order of their acceptability. It is apparent that the range of acceptability from situation to situation is very broad, just as is the range of acceptability from speaker to speaker; and just as the most reputable speakers were found to be the most acceptable, so here the least vociferous modes of expression are preferred.

The percentage of administrators answering "quite permissive" ranged from 25 per cent on the "picketing" question to 75 per cent on the "resolution passed after a referendum" situation. For the "quite permissive" and "fairly permissive" responses, the nine situations seem to fall into four groups of varying acceptability.

Picketing, sit-ins, and resolutions without referenda constitute the least acceptable group. Picketing and sitting-in are both highly visible means of protest. Often they attract considerable publicity, sometimes involve violence, can run afoul of the law, and can be carried out by a small number of dedicated, dissident students who might not have the support of the majority of their peers, not to mention that of the general population. All these factors may contribute to the relative administrative intolerance for these techniques of demonstration. Intolerance for

91

the situation wherein a student government, without a referendum, passes a resolution purporting to speak for the student body probably has a different basis. Administrators may feel that the student government really does not know what the majority of students are thinking on any given situation unless it asks them, and so speaking for the student body is discouraged unless preceded by a referendum. Good evidence exists to support this administrative position: according to their own responses to our questionnaire, most student body presidents did not solicit the views of more than 25 per cent of the student population and many noted that the students themselves would not approve of a resolution without a referendum. It seems fair to assume that an ad-

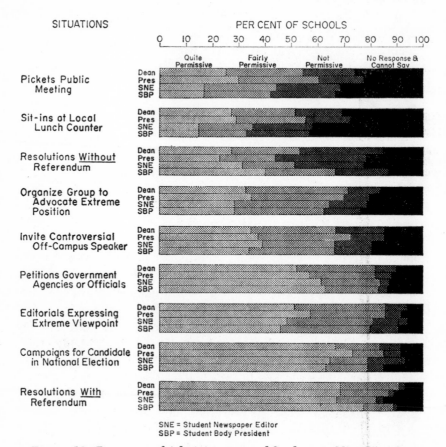

Figure 13. Responses of Administrators and Students to Nine Situations

ministration does not require a referendum simply as a delaying tactic, since the mechanics of polling the student body would give the issue far wider publicity than a simple student government resolution.

The next two items—organizing a group to advocate an extreme position and inviting a controversial off-campus speaker—elicited considerably more permissive responses, especially in the "fairly permissive" category. These two questions both drew about one-third of the responses in the three categories "quite permissive," "fairly permissive," and "cannot say" (or no response). However, administrators' positions on these two issues were more equivocal than their positions on other items. Evidently administrators were not inimical to these actions per se, but they seemed to want very much to know the identity of a speaker or the exact position advocated by the group before they made up their minds; we believe this explains the large response in the median category—"fairly permissive." The responses to the speaker situation provided a check on the much more detailed information elicited in the section of the questionnaire on speakers (presented in Chapter 4). Results obtained on this question were consistent with those described earlier.

On such items as petitioning or taking an extreme editorial stand on a controversial issue, over 80 per cent of administrators reported that they would be quite or fairly permissive. The method of petitioning involves many students, identity is stated, and position is clear. Moreover, petitioning, although it may attract publicity, is seldom illegal, is respectful of constituted authority, almost never involves violence, seems more thoughtful than active, and hence more appropriate to scholars. The writing of a controversial editorial shares these characteristics and although a large number of students are not involved in its production, it has the backing of a hard-working, and presumably responsible, student organization. Student editors and their roles will be discussed in more detail in Chapter 7.

The situations toward which administrators proved most permissive are political campaigning on the campus and the passage of a resolution by the student government after a referendum. Two-thirds of the administrators responded as "quite permissive" to each of these and an additional 15 to 25 per cent reported their position to be "fairly permissive." Since the political campaigning question specified that the candidate was to be running in a national election, and since most such candidates are highly respected men with moderate platforms, such campaigning today must seem innocuous to administrators. The passage of a resolution after a referendum is the most acceptable situation. It involves no illegal or violent activity and the views of a large number of students presumably would be clearly known. Suppression of this democratic, time-honored, and nonviolent technique would seem tyrannical, yet about 10 per cent would be hesitant to permit it.

When we move from the least acceptable situation to those which are more acceptable, the number of administrators who failed to respond diminishes. We might suspect that non-responding administrators were tending to conceal their restrictive impulses if it were not for the fact that students also failed to respond to almost the same degree on each question. Thus, it would seem that for the more controversial techniques, neither students nor administrators know what the administration's policy would be in up to 30 per cent of the colleges. This is probably because the acceptability of these techniques is largely dependent on the timing, purpose, and propriety of their use, and hence blanket policies cannot be formulated.

Agreement of Respondents

On the situations involving picketing, sit-ins, formation of extreme groups, editorials, and campaigning, fewer students estimated administrative permissiveness than did administrators. Invitation of speakers and the passage of a resolution with a referendum received substantially the same responses from students and administrators. However, with regard to petitioning a government agency or publishing a resolution without referendum, students perceived more freedom than did their administrators. The most common pattern—students perceiving less freedom than do administrators—has been interpreted before. Students perceiving more freedom than administrators is the exceptional reaction. In the matter of petitioning, students probably thought it to be a right guaranteed them as citizens. They may have been unaware of the pressure felt by a public university president when his students assault the source of his charter—the government. In regard to publishing a resolution without a referendum, the student respondents may ascribe more prestige to student government than do the administrators, who probably regard the student council, not as a high court, but as a subordinate advisory group. This difference of perspective in assigning prestige may

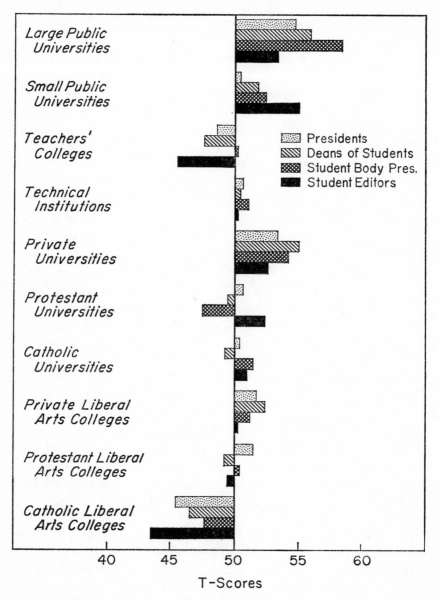

Figure 14. Mean T-Scores on the Situations Factor for Respondent Groups, by Institutional Category

Table 15. Percentage of Respondents, by Institutional Category, Reporting the Administration To Be Quite or Fairly Permissive toward Student Actions

Student Action	Universities					Colleges					
	Large Public	Small Public	Private	Protestant	Catholic	Private	Protestant	Catholic	Teachers'	Technical	All Categories
Picketing	79**	59**	71**	47	58*	63**	44*	36**	39**	47	49
Sit-ins	59**	44	64**	43	48	55**	39*	38**	32**	44	44
Resolution without referendum	82**	67**	67**	51	60	53	52	38**	52	60	54
Organization of group to advocate action	88**	72	62	64	62	78**	67	46**	61**	74	67
Invitation to off-campus speakers	85**	73	89**	72	61*	76**	69	49**	59**	71	68
Petitioning government	88*	80	89*	82	87	86	84	86	75**	72**	82
Controversial editorials	92**	86	92**	84	75**	90**	86	68**	80	90	83
Political campaigning	84	78	88*	91*	85	86*	87**	77**	75**	79	82
Resolution with referendum	89	84	85	77**	83	80**	84*	78**	80**	86	87

* This percentage is significantly different from the percentage for all categories at the .05 level.
** This percentage is significantly different from the percentage for all categories at the .01 level.

sive. Thus, while this method is less sensitive to differences among respondents and does not distinguish "quite" from "fairly" permissive, it has the advantage of discriminating among the nine individual situations. The loss of accuracy from combining response categories is not great. If an individual checked "quite" or "fairly" permissive he can be presumed to perceive more permissiveness than if he failed to respond, or answered negatively.

Results found in this way support those revealed by the technique of factor analysis. That is, the schools are, in order of the most to the least permissive, the large public universities, the private universities and the private liberal arts colleges, and the small public universities. The least permissive schools were the teachers' colleges and, at the bottom, the Catholic liberal arts colleges.

Standing above all other types of schools are the large public universities, which are significantly more permissive than average on every issue except the two most acceptable situations, political campaigning and resolution with referendum. As for political campaigning on the campus, however, private and Protestant universities and liberal arts colleges were significantly more permissive than average. It is unusual that the large public universities, which otherwise have superlative records, should not appear significantly more open than average concerning political campaigning. Perhaps the explanation for this inconsistent finding is that some of these institutions have charter prohibitions about involvement in partisan politics, or administrators may be reluctant to see their students embroiled in politics because they rely on legislatures for their financial support, or government agencies are sources of large research grants. Bearing out this explanation is the fact that the public universities' permissiveness with regard to petitioning of government agencies is only slightly greater than average—significant at the .05 level but not at the .01 level—and also the fact that no other public institutions (small public universities, teachers' colleges, or technical institutions) are more permissive than average concerning either campaigning or petitioning. On the other hand, to say that large public universities are only average in their permissiveness toward political campaigning is not to say that they are restrictive: 84 per cent of these schools rank themselves "quite" or "fairly permissive." Thus, these universities are the most permissive in their attitudes toward the situations in which students demonstrate their views.

Private universities are approximately as open as the large public universities, with some exceptions. On political campaigning and petitioning government agencies they are somewhat more permissive than the large public universities, but still not at the .01 level of statistical significance. The private universities also indicate only average willingness to allow formation of a group to advocate an extreme position. In view of their unusual openness in other areas this is somewhat unexpected, until one considers that what a private university, with a diverse student body and a tradition of free controversy, considers an "extreme" position may be quite different from what other schools—for example a Catholic liberal arts women's college—would consider "extreme." Evidence for this interpretation is cited in Chapter 3 in the discussion of specific student organizations which are active on the campuses. Overcoming the difficulty of incommensurable criteria may be unavoidable where self-appraisal is required and must be considered in interpreting many of the results of this study. In any case, it is clear that private universities show only an average tolerance of groups formed to advocate what seem to the university students and administrators to be "extreme" positions.

Private liberal arts colleges are slightly less permissive. They have less tolerance for resolutions with or without referenda and greater tolerance for groups formed to advocate extreme positions. It would seem that these schools are more tolerant of special-purpose groups, formed to express student opinion on some specific issue, and less tolerant of action by the student government in matters of social controversy. Knowing this, however, does not permit us to infer any less willingness to let students or a group of students formally express their views. It may be only a preference for certain methods or styles.

The small public universities are only slightly more permissive than average, and less permissive than the large public universities or the private universities and liberal arts colleges. They are significantly above average openness on only two situations—picketing, and resolution without referendum. Scores for the technical institutions, the Protestant universities and liberal arts colleges, and the Catholic universities are also close to the mean. The technical institutions (half of which are publicly controlled) diverge significantly from average on only one issue: granting less freedom for petitioning government agencies.

In every case, large schools are more permissive than small schools:

99

this is true whether one contrasts large public universities with small; private universities with liberal arts colleges; Protestant universities with liberal arts colleges; or, especially, the Catholic universities with the liberal arts colleges. Although the Catholic universities are above average on picketing and below average concerning speakers and editorials, the Catholic liberal arts colleges are significantly below average on every issue except petitioning government agencies. It would seem that larger schools are more willing or better able to bear the attacks that come from the outside community when students express themselves demonstratively on divisive social issues.

The teachers' colleges are significantly less permissive than average on seven of the nine situations, the exceptions being resolutions without referenda and editorials on extreme issues. One suspects from this, and from the comments received from student editors at teachers' colleges, that even very bland issues, such as the location of parking lots, can be considered "extreme" at these highly restrictive institutions.

Regional Analysis

Certain regional differences are indicated in Table 16. The middle Atlantic and New England states appear as the most permissive. Each is significantly more open than average on five of the nine responses, although the New England states are significantly less open than average on political campaigning. The West is significantly above the mean in inviting speakers but it is significantly below in allowing political campaigning. Only the southern region is often significantly below the mean. This is the case for picketing, forming a group to advocate an extreme position, inviting off-campus speakers, and petitioning government agencies. Any of these matters could be connected with civil rights but so could any of the others, especially sit-ins, on which the South indicates average permissiveness. To explore further the relationship between civil rights and the South's limited permissiveness, an analysis of responses from Negro and white colleges is necessary; this will be carried out in the next chapter.

Analysis by Sex of Students

Consideration of the effect of the sex of the student body on an institution's permissiveness revealed that on all but two situations men's colleges are more permissive than women's. The two exceptions are res-

Table 16. Percentage of Respondents, by Geographical Region, Reporting the Administration To Be Quite or Fairly Permissive toward Student Actions

Student Action	New England	Middle Atlantic	North Central	North Western	Southern	Western	All Regions
Picketing	60**	52	50	58*	40**	55	49
Sit-ins	52*	49*	42	38	40	44	44
Resolution without referendum	52	60**	56	49	51	55	54
Organization of group to advocate action	74*	71*	66	75*	59**	71	67
Invitation to off-campus speakers ..	78**	71	66	68	58**	79**	68
Petitioning government agencies and officials	85	86*	85**	85	76**	78	82
Editorials about controversial issues	88*	84	82	86	82	82	83
Political campaigning on campus	77*	81	85**	87*	80	73**	82
Resolution with referendum	88	91**	88	82*	85	84	87

* This percentage is significantly different from the percentage for all regions at the .05 level.

** This percentage is significantly different from the percentage for all regions at the .01 level.

olutions with referenda and submission of petitions to government agencies—two of the least active forms of demonstrating student views. This finding is not unexpected in view of the greater limitations placed on women by our society, the more protective attitude of girls' parents and their consequent demands on colleges, and the traditional role of men as risk-takers in the active transformation of society. Coeducational institutions were more free on the average than either men's or women's colleges.

Summary

The freedom for student organizations to engage in demonstrative activity is less clearly relevant to the educational mission of the institution than is free discussion. The extent of this freedom, as of the freedom to invite off-campus speakers, is apparently highly dependent on the purposes, timing, and methods of the demonstration. And the acceptability of demonstrative action varies widely depending upon the technique used. The permissiveness of administrators in allowing their students to demonstrate their views to the outside community seems approximately as great as their permissiveness in allowing speakers to come into the academic world from the outside.

Students perceive only slightly less openness in the policies of their institution than do the administrators. Written policy is in effect at no more than 10 per cent of the schools for any situation except invitation of speakers.

As with free discussion and the invitation of speakers, the most open schools were the large public universities, the private universities, and the private liberal arts colleges; the least open institutions were the Catholic liberal arts colleges and the teachers' colleges. In this case, as in free discussion but unlike speaker invitations, the Catholic universities were of average permissiveness. Also of nearly average permissiveness were the small public universities, the technical institutions, and the Protestant universities and liberal arts colleges.

New England and middle Atlantic states contained a greater proportion of "open" schools than did the other regions, and the southern schools were found to be considerably more restrictive.

The practices of educational institutions in permitting student groups freely to discuss controversial issues, to invite controversial speakers, and to engage in demonstrative activity have been examined. Now, in the next chapter, let us consider a substantive issue which involves the exercise of all three of these freedoms.

6 ✐

Student Freedom and the Civil Rights Issue

THE struggle over civil rights for Negroes has led this nation into a convulsive social revolution, and has also fired the imagination and claimed the energies of the present college generation. Indeed students have played a major role in attempts to resolve this crisis. They have spent summers in Mississippi registering Negro voters, taught in "freedom" schools, and organized and supplied much of the manpower for tutorial programs for deprived Negro children in both the North and the South. They have been prominent in freedom rides, freedom marches, sit-ins, and other demonstrations.

Students' concern about civil rights for Negroes and their intense recent concern about their own civil liberties have emerged almost simultaneously, and it is difficult to say which, if either, interest generated the other. Heirich and Kaplan, in a history of student protest at Berkeley, conclude that during the late fifties both issues were major targets of protest movements on the campus.[1] The authors found that in the University of California at Berkeley, students' concern about their own freedom preceded, and perhaps contributed to, their interest in the Negro civil rights cause. It is not unlikely, however, that on other campuses students may have first committed themselves to action in the civil rights movement, and then found that their freedom to engage in

[1] Max Heirich and Sam Kaplan, "Yesterday's Discord," *California Monthly*, Vol. 75, No. 5 (February 1965), pp. 20–32.

this action was limited by college policy. This discovery, in turn, could have led to an attack on the school policies, and a struggle for students' academic freedom with special emphasis on civil rights. Whatever the historical relationship between the two movements, it is clear that students today are concerned with both: they are asserting not only their interest in civil rights but also their right to be involved in action on this issue and others.

Since Negro civil rights constitutes the most divisive social issue of our times, student engagement in civil rights activities severely tests the permissiveness of college administrators. Thus, the issue will provide us with a most rigorous measure of the extent to which academic freedom for students is actually practiced. It is a substantive issue which may involve exercise of each of the procedural freedoms previously discussed. Are college administrators free enough from external community pressures to grant students freedom to examine both sides of the issue? May students freely speak their convictions concerning civil rights? May students invite civil rights proponents and opponents to speak on campus? In their status as students may they picket, sit in, petition, or otherwise protest in the community?

The Civil Rights Factor

The response choices of all respondents to the questionnaire items examined thus far in our study were subjected to factor analysis—a complex statistical technique which we will not describe here. The assumption is generally made that this analytic method will reduce a large number of variables to a relatively small number of common factors which correspond to the "dimensions of meaning" upon which the respondent's question-answering behavior is based. Thus, we used the method to determine which items respondents tended to answer from a similar or identical perspective.

This analysis extracted six common factors (shown in Figures 19 and 20, Chapter 8) from the forty questionnaire items, and five of these have already been used to organize some of the discussions in preceding chapters. One of the factors was of particular interest to us because it revealed twelve highly loaded items from the sections of the questionnaire on topics, situations, and speakers. The common thread of meaning running through the twelve items in this cluster seemed to be a strong relationship to the civil rights issue. The other twenty-eight items showed neither strong numerical loadings on the factor nor significant substantive relationship to the civil rights issue. We will discuss the factor scores, their alternate meanings, and the scoring method later. First, let us look at the items constituting the factor.

We have examined percentage responses to each of the twelve important items in the civil rights factor in the contexts of previous chapters, but because we are now discussing them as a new gestalt we have grouped them together in Figure 15 for the reader's review. The items receiving high positive weights, by use of a complete multiple regression scoring method, were the situations in which a student organization pickets a public meeting, sits in at a local lunch counter, or sends a petition to a government agency or officials; the discussion of laws prohibiting interracial marriage or local fair housing legislation; and the invitation of Martin Luther King, Robert Moses, or Malcolm X to speak on the campus. The relationship of these items to civil rights is obvious. The negatively weighted items, in order from low to high, were those concerning the invitation of Fred Schwarz, Barry Goldwater, Robert Welch, or George Wallace to speak on the campus. Each of these men has taken a conservative position on civil rights—for example, George Wallace is outspokenly opposed to Negro advancement in an integrated society—thus accounting for the negative weight. Each respondent was assigned a civil rights factor score based on his answers to all forty items—each numerically weighted in terms of its relationship to the civil rights factor. The twelve items listed in Figure 15 accounted for 79 per cent of the score variance. Following this calculation, raw scores were transformed into T-scores (see note on p. 95) to provide a single measure of a respondent's complex of perceptions regarding his school's permissiveness toward topic discussion, speaker invitation, and student action related to civil rights.

Detailed analysis of the T-scores and their relationship to individual item responses revealed that two general response patterns had caused the civil rights items to cluster in the factor analysis. The most evident pattern operated in the following manner: if a respondent perceived his institution to be permissive toward any one of the eight positively weighted items he tended to respond permissively to the other seven positively weighted items and restrictively to the four negatively weighted items, and vice versa. This pattern suggested that the civil rights issue per se and the relevancy of an item to this issue were de-

PER CENT OF SCHOOLS

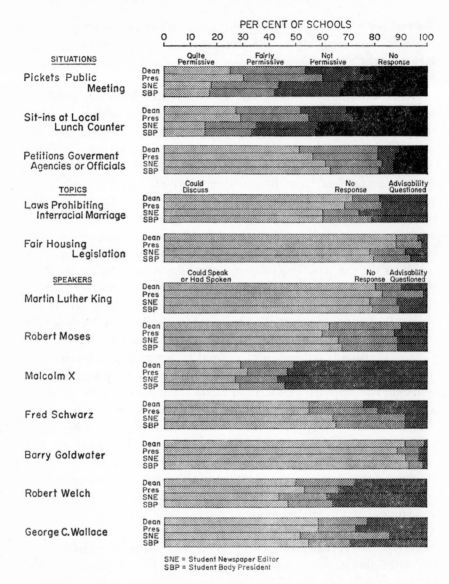

SNE = Student Newspaper Editor
SBP = Student Body President

Figure 15. Responses of Administrators and Students to Questionnaire Items
Related to Civil Rights

termining considerations in the process of response. The second pattern suggested that items were answered by many respondents in terms of their controversiality rather than their relationship to the civil rights issue.

Thus, according to the first pattern certain schools which would approve the discussion of interracial mariage laws, the invitation to Martin Luther King, and the practice of student sit-ins, would also tend to discourage or prohibit the invitation of George Wallace and Robert Welch. Evidently some schools extend their liberality to expressions of the liberal position only. Conversely, some schools admit segregationist speakers but discourage or prohibit integrationist activities, topics, or speakers. In neither of these cases does the school practice true academic freedom since possibilities for opposing opinions and actions are prohibited.

The first pattern is not evident in Figure 15, but the graph does show, in accordance with the second pattern, the broad range of controversiality and institutional freedom. As we have noted elsewhere, the topics, situations, and speakers which would attract the greatest unfavorable publicity, which would seem least academic in quality, and which would lead to the greatest probability of acts of violence were perceived as least acceptable to college administrations. Also, the most controversial of our questionnaire items were related to the civil rights issue. The reader will recall, for example, that sitting-in and picketing were the two least acceptable modes of student expression, and the least acceptable discussion topic was laws prohibiting interracial marriage. Likewise, Malcolm X was considered by our respondents to be one of the highly controversial speakers. But not all civil rights items were highly controversial: our respondents viewed petitioning as an appropriate method of expressing viewpoints, and Barry Goldwater and Martin Luther King—despite their diverse positions on civil rights—were both clearly acceptable as speakers. For those who answered according to the second pattern, the difference in acceptability of Martin Luther King and Malcolm X seemed to be based more on their respective methods or reputations, or the cogency of their arguments than on their opinions about civil rights. Both men (before the death of Malcolm X) envisioned a major revolution in the practices of society and sought immediate change. Martin Luther King strives as energetically and fearlessly for his goals as did Malcolm X for his, but in very different ways.

The degree of controversiality, then, was certainly a second response determinant.

The civil rights factor scores thus reflected two response patterns— one based on an item's relationship to civil rights, and the other based on the item's controversiality. The highest factor scores indicate that respondents saw their institutions as encouraging pro-civil rights activities and discouraging segregationist speakers. Slightly lower scores were obtained by respondents in colleges that encouraged pro-civil rights activities more than most colleges while taking average positions on anti-civil rights speakers. A somewhat lower, but still above average, score resulted for the respondent who envisioned his college as relatively open to all sides of the civil rights question. The lowest factor scores were calculated for those individuals who said their institutions permitted as speakers opponents of civil rights but prohibited proponents of the movement or activities of students in favor of Negro rights. A respondent who reported his school to be closed to any activity related to civil rights—no matter what positions were expressed—received a score below the average but not as low as the respondent in an anti-civil rights school. The factor scores do not in themselves reveal which of these alternate patterns of response, or what combination of patterns, determined the score. They indicate only in a general way whether respondents saw their schools as more or less friendly to civil rights, and/or opposed to its opponents, than did others.

Two types of analysis are presented here in order to determine where student academic freedom, as it relates to the civil rights issue, is practiced. First, the factor scores in Figure 16 show in which types of schools civil rights freedom or lack of freedom is observed. Second, to determine the significance and subtle meanings in these findings it is necessary to analyze the responses from each category of institution to each of the twelve items which constitute the factor. Differences between the percentage responses and the factor scores may arise in three ways. First, the percentages are less discriminating than the factor scores. In tables of percentages permissive responses are compared with all other responses, rather than weighted differentially for a "quite permissive" or "fairly permissive" response; and, unlike the factor scores, no distinction is made between the "not permissive" or "cannot say" response and a failure to respond at all. Second, the factor scores did not weight each of the twelve items equally; rather each item was weighted in proportion to the specific factor loading and partial multiple regression weight derived for the item. Third, the twenty-eight "residual" items had a small effect on the factor scores depending on their numerical relationships to the factor. Thus, the civil rights factor scores are highly discriminating but somewhat ambiguous, while the percentage responses have the advantage of supplying simple results with respect to individual items but oversimplify the relationships. Factor scores and statistically significant percentage differences will be used together in subsequent interpretations.

Analysis by Institutional Category

Figure 16 shows which respondents from each type of institution reported more permissive or more restrictive policies toward civil rights than the average. The average is represented by a score of 50. According to these data, the large public universities and the private and Catholic universities and liberal arts colleges appear favorable to the civil rights movement, while the Protestant schools and teachers' colleges and, to a lesser extent, the technical institutions and small public universities are less partisan to this current issue.

Responses to the twelve civil rights items varied widely among the different types of institutions, and give meaning to the general findings presented in Figure 16. First, let us examine the five types of institutions which were more partisan in favor of civil rights and/or opposed to its opponents than the other schools. The responses of these schools—the large public, Catholic, and private universities and the private and Catholic liberal arts colleges—are shown in Table 17.

Both the large public universities and the private universities were significantly above the mean in permissiveness with respect to every issue, situation, and speaker associated with civil rights, pro or con. The private universities were somewhat more biased in favor of the proponents of this issue, and hence received a higher score. But in both cases, students had a greater than average freedom to deal with the several facets of the civil rights issue and to align themselves with any position.

Catholic universities were more permissive than average with respect to picketing by students and discussion of local fair housing legislation by student groups. They were significantly less permissive than average with regard to a proposed invitation to Malcolm X, but

109

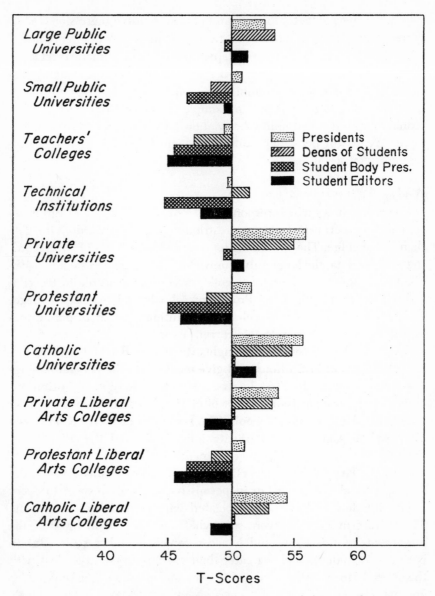

Figure 16. Mean T-Scores on the Civil Rights Factor for Respondent Groups, by Institutional Category

Table 17. Percentage of Respondents, by Five Types of Institution, Indicating Greater than Average Permissiveness toward Civil Rights Items

Item	Large Public Universities	Private Schools		Catholic Schools		All Schools
		Univer-sities	Liberal Arts	Univer-sities	Liberal Arts	
Situations						
Picketing	79**	71**	63**	58*	36**	49
Sit-ins	59**	64**	55**	48	38**	44
Petitioning	88*	89*	86	87	86*	82
Topics						
Marriage laws	76**	81**	72*	70	62*	66
Fair housing	92**	89*	85	90**	81	82
Speakers						
Martin Luther King...	85*	92**	84*	85	83	80
Robert Moses	81**	87**	76**	61	51**	64
Malcolm X	56**	69**	46**	12**	10**	30
Fred Schwarz	80**	80**	73**	46**	44**	59
Barry Goldwater	96*	96*	94	90	90	92
Robert Welch	78**	80**	64**	38*	20**	48
George Wallace	88**	77**	71**	30**	19**	55

* This percentage is significantly different from the percentage for all schools at the .05 level.
** This percentage is significantly different from the percentage for all schools at the .01 level.

not with regard to one to Martin Luther King or Robert Moses. Thus, they showed a slight bias in favor of the proponents of civil rights in situations and topics and a slight negative bias on speakers. Malcolm X, however, had a low factor loading, indicating that for our respondents he was only peripherally associated with the civil rights movement. Therefore, the opposition of Catholic universities to Malcolm X was heavily discounted in the weighting process, and these schools received a positive score for their attitude toward civil rights proponents. In their attitude toward the opponents of civil rights Catholic universities proved to be highly negative and this further increased their score. They opposed the invitation of Fred Schwarz, Robert Welch, and Governor Wallace, and they showed only average tolerance toward the invitation of Barry Goldwater. Although the Catholic universities provided less academic freedom for their students, by limiting their right to hear the opponents of civil rights, they obtained a higher score than the large public or private universities through their bias in favor of civil rights. For these schools freedom tended to be one-dimensional in that the student group which advocated civil rights would be approved while the student group which opposed civil rights would more often be evaluated as violating the college rules. Although this tendency is significant and real, it must be remembered that it is a slight one and does not characterize all Catholic universities.

The Catholic and private liberal arts colleges both scored as advocates of Negro civil rights. The Catholic institutions achieved this score even though they were restrictive with respect to eight of the twelve relevant items and significantly permissive on only one. These schools were not practitioners of academic freedom for civil rights supporters, but they restricted the opponents and hence received a positive score. Of the four speakers taking conservative stands toward Negro rights, they restricted three significantly more than the average of other institutions, while of the eight pro-civil rights items, they restricted five significantly more than average, and one less. The private liberal arts colleges were also classified as supporters of civil rights, but they favored the proponents and opponents about equally, being permissive toward three or four of each set of items. Their positive score resulted from the fact that there were more items on the pro-civil rights side of the ledger in our measuring criterion, their support of each of these was greater, and the distribution of "fairly" versus "quite" permissive responses was more heavily weighted toward the pro-civil rights speakers.

In summary, the private institutions and the large public universities are centers of academic freedom on the civil rights issue, allowing liberty to debaters on either side of the issue. The liberties appear to be slightly greater for those who advocate civil rights. The Catholic liberal arts colleges oppose the enemies of civil rights, but tend not to encourage its advocates more than average. They simply discourage the proponents less often than the opponents. Catholic universities, on the other hand, generally permit pro- but not anti-civil rights activities and speakers.

Now, let us consider the groups of schools which show a less than average bias in favor of civil rights. These are, in the order of the most to the least restrictive, the teachers' colleges, the Protestant universities and liberal arts colleges, the technical institutions, and the small public universities. The responses of these five groups of schools are summarized in Table 18.

The teachers' colleges are significantly restrictive concerning all of the

112

Table 18. Percentage of Respondents, by Five Types of Institution, Indicating
Less than Average Permissiveness toward Civil Rights Items

| Item | Tech- nical | Small Public University | Protestant Schools | | Teachers' Colleges | All Schools |
			Univer- sities	Liberal Arts		
Situations						
Picketing	47	59**	47	44*	39**	49
Sit-ins	44	44	43	39*	32**	44
Petitioning	72**	80	82	84	75**	82
Topics						
Marriage laws	64	64	54**	61*	60**	66
Fair housing	81	84	84	80	77**	82
Speakers						
Martin Luther King...	74	79	77	76*	69**	80
Robert Moses	57	66	48**	64	54**	64
Malcolm X	32	35	28	20**	22**	30
Fred Schwarz	50	66*	61	58	50**	59
Barry Goldwater	89	93	95	94	86**	92
Robert Welch	48	65**	45	42**	38**	48
George Wallace	56	73**	62	56	54	55

* This percentage is significantly different from the percentage for all schools at
the .05 level.
** This percentage is significantly different from the percentage for all schools
at the .01 level.

items but one, the invitation of Governor Wallace. Also, they are less
restrictive toward the opponents than toward the proponents of civil
rights. Hence, their negative score.

The Protestant institutions are significantly more negative than average toward a few of these items, more often those that are pro- rather
than anti-civil rights. The reader is again cautioned to remember that
there are more pro- than anti-civil rights items. The technical institutions are in much the same situation, scoring significantly negative on
only one item, the freedom to petition.

The small public universities are not significantly restrictive on any
of these items, but they are significantly permissive toward only one
of the pro-civil rights items, and toward three of the anti-civil rights
speakers. Thus, their policies appear to have a bias against civil rights,
although this is slight.

In summarizing this section a distinction must be re-emphasized.
Some schools permit their students academic freedom in the area of
civil rights—that is, permit students to work for civil rights and to invite speakers who advocate civil rights, and also allow them to invite

113

and listen to those who attack the movement. These schools include the private institutions, the large public universities, and to a lesser degree, the small public universities. The types of schools which tend not to permit this sort of freedom are the Catholic liberal arts colleges, the teachers' colleges, and to a much lesser degree, the Protestant institutions and Catholic universities. Whether specific schools tend to be biased for or against civil rights is an entirely different question and leads to the following answers: the Catholic universities seem to have a slightly greater bias in favor of civil rights liberals than other institutions, and the Protestant institutions and small public universities seem to be slightly biased in favor of civil rights conservatives.

Regional Differences

Long before the Civil War, rights for Negroes was a regional issue in the United States. Now the Negro population is still located principally in the South but associated social, political, and economic problems have long since erupted in northern and western cities. The student drive to improve the condition of Negroes in the North has come largely from northern college students working on educational projects in their local communities. In the South this impetus has come from the southern Negro college students and in part from northern students making forays into the South. Martin Oppenheimer found, in his investigation of 1960 sit-ins, that the presence of a Negro college was one of the major factors associated with the appearance of civil rights activities.[2]

In order to determine whether limitations on civil rights activities were greater for college students in one section of the country than another, we analyzed by regions the responses to the twelve civil-rights-related items. Table 19 indicates for each geographical region whether the freedom accorded to students concerning each of the twelve issues is greater or less than the average freedom on that issue for all schools. The table does not show whether students are content with the degree of freedom which they enjoy.

In the New England region, students may participate in six of the eight pro-civil rights activities and listen to two of the four anti-civil rights speakers significantly more than the average student. New Eng-

[2] Martin Oppenheimer, "Institutions of Higher Learning and the 1960 Sit-ins: Some Clues for Social Action," *Journal of Negro Education*, June 1963, pp. 286–288.

Table 19. Percentage of Respondents, by Geographical Region, Indicating
Permissiveness toward Civil Rights Items

Item	New England	Middle Atlantic	North Central	North Western	Southern	Western	All Regions
Situations							
Picketing	60**	52	50	58*	40**	55	49
Sit-ins	52*	49*	42	38	40	44	44
Petitioning	85	86*	85**	85	76**	78	82
Topics							
Marriage laws ..	77**	72**	67	72	49**	66	66
Fair housing ...	86	85	82	86	78*	86	82
Speakers							
Martin Luther King	91**	87**	84**	90**	55**	76	80
Robert Moses ...	74**	74**	65	64	45**	72*	64
Malcolm X	54**	38**	26**	29	14**	46**	30
Fred Schwarz ..	62	62	59	64	49**	78**	59
Barry Goldwater	92	93	93	98**	86**	94	92
Robert Welch ..	60**	54**	46	60**	33**	60**	48
George Wallace.	64**	55	55	64*	50*	61	55

* This percentage is significantly different from the percentage for all regions at
the .05 level.
** This percentage is significantly different from the percentage for all regions
at the .01 level.

land colleges clearly permit the greatest over-all freedom concerning
civil rights issues. Colleges in the middle Atlantic states also allow substantial freedom regarding these issues although, unlike New England,
permissiveness on an invitation to Governor Wallace is not significantly
greater than average. In the Northwest and West there is slightly greater
than average freedom for students both for and against civil rights, and
in the North Central region freedom regarding civil rights activities is
about at the average for the nation.

In the South there is less than average freedom on seven of the eight
pro-civil-rights items. However, all four speakers who are conservative
about civil rights are less often welcome than the average for the nation. There is no evidence in our data that southern schools *as a group*
are biased against civil rights.

Despite the Supreme Court's May 1954 ruling about the integration
of public schools, there still exist many institutions in the South with a
predominantly Negro enrollment and others whose students are, with
few exceptions, white. There are also such colleges outside the South,
in the so-called border states, although in some cases an institution may

be composed predominantly of white students only because there are fewer qualified Negro candidates residing in the geographical area it serves. It is likely that colleges with Negro students take an entirely different attitude toward civil rights issues than do colleges with white students. All of the country's Negro colleges were compared with white colleges with respect to the issues considered in this report, and the following conclusions were reached.

Negro institutions showed more than the average change in the climate of student expression. Their students displayed more interest in controversial issues than was observed elsewhere, as well as a greater tendency to demonstrate this interest in visible and voluble ways. The educational philosophy of Negro institutions was found to be more liberal than that of most other institutions. But although Negro college administrators more frequently defended students' rights in the abstract, they were less permissive than average in granting students these freedoms. In discussion of controversial topics, invitation of controversial speakers, and participation in demonstrative situations, students in Negro colleges were significantly less free than those in white institutions. If the speaker was highly reputable, however, as defined in Chapter 4, there was no significant difference between the Negro colleges and others. If the topic for discussion was religious in nature then the Negro schools were significantly more free. And on the civil rights measure the Negro colleges were far more free, strikingly high in view of the fact that the Negro colleges are less often free with regard to topics, speakers, and situations in general. Thus, Negro colleges tend to be conservative and restrictive educational institutions, yet these schools are associated with the civil rights cause to the extent of reversing their apparent general policy of noninvolvement with societal issues.

Conservatism may seem the safest course for a Negro institution. Since Negro schools, particularly those in the South, tend to receive a disproportionate amount of criticism for involvement in controversy, it may be that establishment and preservation of a reputable image is of paramount importance. Civil rights activism is the exception. A Negro college which divorced itself from the concerns of its race might justly be accused of unprincipled submission to the system which has nourished an inferior and segregated education for Negroes. On the other hand, commitment to the civil rights cause involves real dangers to a Negro college strongly supported financially by the local white community, and may interfere as well with the broad educational aims of the institution, if students plunge directly into involvement that precludes detachment and objectivity.

Table 20 provides a closer examination of the responses of southern Negro colleges to the twelve civil rights items, contrasting their responses with those of southern white colleges. Negro schools are clearly much more permissive toward the issues associated with civil rights than are southern white colleges. The exception to this is the expressive technique of petitioning government agencies. Since petitioning involves listing the names of the petitioners, this might be considered a very dangerous action because of the possibility of reprisals by extremist groups getting possession of the list. Also, petitions are likely to identify the petitioners as students of a particular college. Finally, petitioning white officials in the established local governments probably has been found to have little effect.

Southern Negro colleges tend to be slightly less permissive than the white colleges with regard to invitations to conservative civil rights speakers, although statistical tests indicate that these differences are not significant even at the .05 level. That is, it is possible that they are the result of chance statistical variation. Nonetheless, it can be said that

Table 20. Percentage of Permissive Responses to Civil Rights Items for Schools with Negro and White Students in the Southern Region

Item	Predominantly Negro Enrollment	Predominantly White Enrollment	Difference
Situations			
Picketing	67	36	31**
Sit-ins	82	30	52**
Petitioning	71	77	6
Topics			
Marriage laws	71	44	27*
Fair housing	85	75	10
Speakers			
Martin Luther King	92	47	45**
Robert Moses	77	40	37**
Malcolm X	30	10	20*
Fred Schwarz	43	52	9
Barry Goldwater	78	89	11
Robert Welch	23	36	13
George Wallace	32	54	22

* The difference between Negro and white schools is significant at the .05 level.
** The difference between Negro and white schools is significant at the .01 level.

the responding southern Negro colleges are consistently less willing to hear Wallace, Welch, Goldwater, and Schwarz than are the responding southern white colleges.

It was found earlier that the southern schools were less permissive than average with regard to those activities which favored civil rights and those speakers who opposed it. Now it is possible to make a further distinction. In regard to the issues, speakers, and activities favoring the civil rights movement, southern Negro colleges are more permissive than the average of all schools, while southern white colleges are distinctly less permissive. As for the speakers who have adopted conservative positions on civil rights, they are slightly more acceptable at southern white schools than elsewhere in the country, but they are distinctly less acceptable at the southern Negro institutions. Thus, although the South on the average is only slightly more restrictive with regard to both sides of the civil rights issue than the rest of the country, the southern white schools are much more restrictive on the items favoring civil rights, and the southern Negro schools are more restrictive concerning speakers opposing this movement. The civil rights issue enlists the partisan support of colleges in the South, and it is rare to find southern institutions which permit their students the freedom to choose sides. This is scarcely surprising, but it provides a documented example of the possible danger to education of too great an involvement of the university in the community: the atmosphere of objectivity is likely to be lost if the college itself encourages a partisan role. Given the depth of feeling about the civil rights issue in the South, the involvement of individuals on one side or the other of the problem, and the de facto segregated nature of the southern educational system itself, such a development is probably inevitable.

Responses from southern schools were further analyzed by institutional category to identify the most marked divergences between Negro and white institutions. It was discovered that the predominantly white Protestant liberal arts colleges and teachers' colleges scored as least permissive of all institutions with regard to pro-civil rights activities. But just the opposite occurred among predominantly Negro colleges. Protestant liberal arts and teachers' colleges with Negro students are the two types of institutions with the highest scores for promoting civil rights activities.

We have talked about Negro and white institutions, northern and

118

southern schools, public and private universities, and sectarian and non-sectarian schools. These are only convenient and meaningful groupings for presenting data: individual schools in each of these categories embrace widely divergent philosophies and practices. Nowhere is this more true than in the present discussion of attitudes toward civil rights. "Average" behavior is a composite of many different kinds of activity. No single institution resembles the "southern white school" point for point; no Negro school conforms to the patterns of the average of Negro institutions.

Although the majority of Negro institutions tend to interpret students' rights conservatively (unless students are directing their action toward civil rights), there are noticeably liberal Negro institutions in the South. Supporting broad student freedoms, the president of Paine College issued this public statement: "Without question a student who enrolls in a private college voluntarily identifies himself with its ideals, becomes by choice, subject to its rules and disciplines, as well as to its instructions and standards. He does not thereby surrender to the college a right to govern his entire being, to control his thinking, or to determine the manner in which he exercises his responsibility as a free citizen in a political democracy."[3]

A Paine College student has freedom extending far beyond the area of civil rights, according to the president: he may exercise whatever rights are ensured by his status as a citizen. But while the majority of Negro institutions allow their students to participate in civil rights activities, there are some which remain silent and inactive. Fear of the surrounding community may check freedom, as is illustrated by the difficulties which one institution has in granting its students the freedom to participate in civil rights activities.

A small Protestant Negro liberal arts college in a southern city of average size is a poignant example. Students in this college are allowed considerable freedom of speech as long as they do nothing that will antagonize local white citizens. The dean states, "Because this college is financed by white southerners, and because it is located in a stronghold of the Ku Klux Klan and the White Citizens Councils, the activity of our students in the current protest movement has been sporadic. They have been requested not to 'rock the boat,' not only because of the water

[3] E. Clayton Calhoun, "A Calm Address to Men of Decency and Reason," *Augusta Chronicle*, December 18, 1960.

(which is everywhere), but mainly because of the sharks which infest this particular water (KKK and WCC)." This is a dramatic illustration of the pressures of a hostile environment and how these pressures limit students' freedom to act on the issue of civil rights. This school receives the financial support of the white citizens of the local community but will continue to do so only so long as college policies do not disturb the "separate but equal" doctrine that has given it sustenance.

Both the president and the dean of the college express emphatic agreement with a liberal philosophy of student freedom, but fear determines their decisions, as they readily admit. The dean confides, "We agonize over each proposal of a speaker with controversial convictions." The president adds that the criterion for permitting a speaker is the degree to which it is anticipated he will inflame the local populace. Radicals and conservatives alike have been banned from the campus: "We tend to take the safe course in any situation," observed the student newspaper editor. When students at the college wanted to invite a representative of the Student Nonviolent Coordinating Committee (S.N.C.C.) to speak before them, they resorted to an elaborate subterfuge. The representative, although he never appeared on campus, "spoke"—through the dean, reading his speech from a manuscript.

The president and dean agreed that students at this college have an energetic interest in the major issues of the day but very little outlet for their concern. The dissatisfaction of these students may be read in the comments of the student newspaper editor: "We can *discuss* anything. It is generally o.k. to have opinions as long as they are not too radical and everyone can agree with you, smile, and forget it." The dean of students laments that his city is neither large enough nor small enough to allow him or his students freedom of movement since, as he said, ". . . we are located neither in the isolation of a village nor in the isolation of a metropolis, but in the involvement of a small city."

Martin Oppenheimer[4] has pointed out that the majority of sit-ins in the South have occurred in large cities. A Negro college in a large city is somewhat insulated by the very size and diversity of the city. Its integrationist activities might be supported by a major segment of the city's population, or perhaps go unnoticed. And in a small town public opinion would probably lack potency. But the particular college we have

[4] Oppenheimer, *loc. cit.*

been discussing is neither shielded nor isolated from unfriendly public opinion. The presence of a college is thus of major interest to the community; if it happens to be a Negro institution in a hostile southern white community, its activities are likely to be under constant scrutiny and surveillance.

The plight of this particular college is an illustration of what can happen when schools everywhere are not free to grant desired freedoms to their students. Clearly the educational mission of all institutions of higher learning ought to be the elimination of fear and prejudice. Freedom to advance the cause of civil rights (or any other cause) on a college campus can only exist when the rights of the college in the community have been assured. An institution cannot accord its students the freedom to participate in civil rights activities *or any other controversial activities* when its own institutional rights are denied.

Southern white institutions, on the average, have been shown to be restrictive concerning all civil-rights-related activities, and particularly concerning pro-civil rights activities. While this may be true, in general, it must be remembered that there are exceptions. Some white students in southern institutions have taken their place beside their northern counterparts in some freedom marches and demonstrations. Although white students from the South are less often permitted to participate in civil rights activities, some are active members of the various civil rights groups. As an example of changing social consciousness, students at the University of Alabama have recently formed a Human Rights Forum, an attempt to reach beneath hostility to a genuine understanding of the issues at stake in this contemporary human struggle for equality.

Moreover, one small Catholic girls' school in the South contradicts nearly every generalization made thus far about Catholic liberal arts colleges and about southern white institutions. Not only do the administrators of this particular college express an attitude of great permissiveness, but the dean of students laments that her girls have failed to utilize fully their opportunities. Indeed she reports that she would like to see more dissent on campus, not less. While Catholic liberal arts colleges were observed to tolerate civil-rights-related activities at about the average level, and southern white institutions were less free than average, this particular Catholic, white southern college scores high among those institutions whose students exercise freedom to participate in civil-rights-related activities. The freedom of students in this school is greater than at the majority of Catholic institutions: these students are also granted freedom to hear conservative positions expressed. This small and outspokenly permissive school is a caution to those who would generalize to *all* schools data which only describe *most* schools.

One further such example may be cited. In another southern institution, a large Protestant university with predominantly white enrollment, all five respondents agreed that nearly all the topics, speakers, and situations listed on the questionnaire would be acceptable at their institution. Students could advocate unpopular views on interracial marriage; they could picket or sit in; they had formed a civil rights organization on campus; the student newspaper editor had written editorials promoting civil rights for Negroes. The student editor, like his administrators, had received much bitter censure for his stands; but he had not been censored. Martin Luther King had spoken at this school, bringing heavy criticism from such groups as the KKK. The student newspaper editor indicated that Earl Warren could speak but added that he "might be picketed; very unpopular." The hostility of the environment makes the liberalism of this institution all the more impressive. Its record matches that of the most liberal northern universities.

Summary

The civil rights movement has in part been led by college students, and in providing this leadership they have tested the permissiveness of their institutions. They have involved themselves and their schools in divisive and at times dangerous social controversy, and have sometimes substituted engagement for objectivity.

The private institutions, the large public universities, and to a lesser degree the small public universities, permitted their students more than average freedom concerning civil rights activities—both pro and con. The Catholic liberal arts colleges, teachers' colleges, and to a lesser degree the Protestant institutions and Catholic universities tended to permit less than average freedom on these issues. The Catholic universities seemed to be slightly favorable to civil rights and the Protestant institutions and small public universities appeared to be slightly favorable to the conservative civil rights speakers.

In the South, the Negro colleges permit activity favorable to civil rights, and tend to discourage that which is opposed, while the tendency for white institutions is in the opposite direction. In general, there is less permissiveness here for the objective examination of this issue than elsewhere in the nation. While this may be the case, it is increasingly unjustifiable to single out the South as the only villain in the civil rights drama. Considerable progress has been made as responsible citizens recognize their duty to shape the laws of the land and to adhere to them. A few southern educational institutions are, as we have shown, among the nation's most liberal institutions.

Having considered the change in the campus climate, the educational philosophy of administrators, and the actual practices of student freedom, we turn in the next chapter to a consideration of the students whose pivotal positions might permit them to influence the administrators of colleges to alter present policies.

7

The Role of Student Leaders

THE limits of several types of academic freedom have been delineated. It is unlikely that those limits will be widened through the autonomous action of most administrators or as the result of violent, undisciplined student demonstrations. It seems to us that the boundaries of student academic freedom can best be set through consultation among administrators and those students in a position to represent fairly and argue cogently in behalf of the needs of students. In order to determine just what the position of student leaders is, vis-à-vis students and administrators, information was gathered on the functions and responsibilities of the newspaper editor, the student body president, and those students involved in college policy-making.

Where student body presidents and student newspaper editors maintain their independence and students are permitted a voice in policy-making committees, three effects will probably be observed. First, students will be in a more powerful position to persuade the administration to grant the freedom they desire than is true at institutions where student leaders are censored or ignored. Second, administrators may find it easier to gain support for their policies when students have a hand in formulating policy than when they receive it as a *fait accompli*. Finally, if channels of communication are open between students and administrators, this is likely to lead to a more rational resolution of conflict than in the case where each party is operating in the dark, unaware of the

124

other's intentions until they are crystallized into exasperating, and often irrational, action. As one of our administrator respondents said, "An hour of talks beforehand is worth twenty hours afterward."

Editorial Freedom

The student newspaper editor is seldom a free agent. At half the schools he claims to be responsible to a faculty adviser, who is in turn responsible to the president for the supervision of the student newspaper and its editorial content. At about 15 per cent of the schools the editor is responsible to the dean of students or to the head of the journalism department, and 30 per cent of the schools to a publications board (which in 70 per cent of the cases has one or more faculty members).

Although the deans report that in 26 per cent of the schools they are directly responsible for supervising the student newspaper, the student editors are aware of this at only 10 per cent of the institutions. Evidently the dean's supervision is exercised so subtly and inoffensively that most student editors do not perceive the official channels of responsibility. At 15 per cent of the schools, however, the dean or a member of his staff attends routine meetings with the student editor to discuss editorial policies.

The budget of the newspaper is controlled by the student government organization in 30 per cent of the schools, and by the publications board at 18 per cent. The faculty adviser holds the purse strings at about 20 per cent of the schools while the dean, head of the journalism department, or chairman of the student affairs committee performs this function at another 15 per cent. Budget control was either distributed among several groups or not reported in the remaining 17 per cent of the schools. Hence, students themselves have direct *control* of the budget in only one-third of the schools.

Newspaper sales account for a very small part of the budget: at 85 per cent of the schools sales provided less than 10 per cent of the revenue. Sale of advertisements is also insufficient at most schools: this source of funds supplied more than half of the newspaper's budget at only 15 per cent of the institutions. Although almost all school newspapers derive some revenue from subscriptions and advertisements, this must be supplemented in nearly every case by funds from the college's operating budget, or incidental fees collected from students by the college. At almost half the colleges more than 50 per cent of the budget was supplied by incidental fees, and at one-fourth the college's operating budget supplied more than half the newspaper's funds.

In most colleges, then, the source of necessary funds for operation of the newspaper is the administration and the student editor is held responsible to a faculty member or administrator who in turn is responsible to the president for the supervision of the newspaper. The editor is clearly not independent in the institutional hierarchy, and the university holds power with which to impose censorship and control. Is this power used?

The student editor at each institution was asked about various forms of censorship and censure which he might have experienced, and he was given ample opportunity to describe more subtle forms of control. The deans were asked similar questions.

Some of the editors reported that they enjoyed almost complete freedom. One said,

The editor may say just about anything he pleases about any issue—school or otherwise, within the limits of the law.

One editor had found allies among the students:

Advertisers have said "liberal" stands will lead to decrease in ads but student Senate promises to make up any differences—more ads are being sold now than ever before.

Another editor described a responsible, but not restrictive, system:

The editors compose the editorial policy under which they will operate for the year they are in office. The editor and advisors sign this. It is then presented to the Dean of Students for her information—*not* her approval.

At another school responsibility is borne individually instead of collectively:

Any editorial opinion expressed by the editor or any member of the staff which is not shared by the rest of the sub-editors must be a signed editorial and is to be considered the opinion of only the individual whose name it bears.

The same editor later commented on his own experience with this practice:

There are always the quizzical stares, the horrible glares, and mutterings of such words as "fink" to cope with. But nothing too unsettling.

Some editors felt unrestrained by the administration, but mentioned the requirements imposed by responsible journalism:

None [no restrictions] in particular; but in dealing with campus activities *all* areas must be investigated before stating an opinion because students and administration are quick to criticize—although this is *not* a restriction.

Another editor said he felt no formal pressure, but that he "might occasionally get a call from a faculty member or student who disagrees, suggesting that I have holes in my head."

The editors who wrote these replies were not suffering under the heavy hand of an administrative censor. Instead, they were simply feeling the slings and arrows of outraged readers, a hazard common to their chosen calling.

There was a second set of answers which suggested that the editor felt not only that he was limited by his good taste and judgment, but also that the administration was keeping a careful and restrictive eye on him and his publication. These editors did not feel oppressed beyond endurance but they felt limited. One said:

The editor is advised not to say anything that will downgrade the school. He has considerable freedom within this area.

A second asserted:

We are expected to omit from our publication any article, picture, etc. that would fail to represent Catholic attitudes.

One knew that it was taboo to "criticize the Board of Regents, or admit the existence of the word or genders 'sex.'" Another asserted he could not "use such words as Beer, Wine, Suds, or any other term frequently used in reference to alcoholic beverages—not in news or advertising."

These restrictions reflect a role conflict for the collegiate newspaper. At some institutions it is expected to serve as a means for disseminating news and opinion not only among the immediate college community of students and faculty but also among regents, alumni, potential students, parents, and other interested parties. For a relatively obscure school the student paper may serve as the primary means by which the college is known to the outside community, and so attacking the evils of the institution may seem an act of disloyalty unless, or even although, the institution's advantages are also touted by the paper. The problem here is that the two functions are incompatible—students do not want the newspaper to be a public relations gimmick, and alumni and parents want to know about everything that goes on, not just what the student editor thinks needs correcting. Perhaps the moral is that colleges should have newspapers and news bulletins.

A third group of editors not only felt restricted but reported they were subject to tyrannical and arbitrary oppression. One said:

The phantom figure of the president hangs over the institution—the editor can't get too liberal or the phantom might materialize in the flesh.

When asked about subtle forms of censorship, the same editor said:

The only subtle thing around here is the phantom figure of Our Leader, and that's about as subtle as an elephant doing a mambo.

Another editor said:

No part of the paper may criticize faculty or administration individually or collectively, directly or indirectly. Criticism of rules and regulations is not permitted. Criticism of student conditions is frowned upon.

A stringent criterion of censorship was described by one student:

Any editorial or story which, in the opinion of the President, or the faculty sponsor, is damaging to the college is censored or not even discussed in the paper.

A less explicit, but potentially even more stringent, criterion was this:

The reason generally given for the rejection of editorials on controversial issues is that they are just not "collegiate." The decision is somewhat arbitrary based on the particular biases of the faculty adviser.

These editors clearly knew the limits to their freedom, or rather they knew who would be setting the limits and in some cases what criteria would be used. They also had a clear idea of what would happen should the limits by transgressed. One expressed the school's traditional policy:

The dean of students will expel from school any editor printing articles which he has been ordered not to print.

At another school,

Last year's editor was given "one more strike and you're out of the ball game" threats after two previous trips to the president's office.

At another institution punishment was meted out less directly:

The dean is highly influential on the committee which determines a student's academic standing. It is thus inadvisable to attack directly certain institutional follies if the editor's academic record is not absolutely spotless.

A threat of this nature, if accurately represented, scarcely seems appropriate to an institution of higher education.

Students are not always ready to submit to administrative fiat. One thoughtful editor complained that his paper had become an extension of the alumni magazine. He then told the story of his revolt:

During the past year the newspaper attempted to broaden its service by raising controversial topics. Each new issue that was raised and the "fight" which was generally required to get the article printed extended the possibilities open to the paper—essentially policy was being formed. This effort, though, was composed of a number of "test cases," each one more or less testing just how far the paper could go before the heavy hand of the administration curbed such attempts. Instead of an atmosphere of openness, the paper was published in an atmosphere of "will this be censored or passed?" Such an atmosphere is not conducive to good journalism as it could breed sensationalism for its own sake.

A person so conscious of the dangers inherent in his own revolt—not to himself but to his cause of good journalism—is an impressive individual. One would think that such an editor could be trusted to print a thoughtful, responsible paper.

Statistically, how often are editors censored? At 42 per cent of American colleges, editors are required to submit copy to someone before publication. In 75 per cent of those cases that person was the faculty adviser to the student newspaper. Submission of copy does not necessarily imply censorship. However, 35 per cent of the editors who had to submit copy reported that censorship had actually occurred against their wishes as compared with only 4 per cent of those not required to submit editorial copy for review. A total of 15 per cent of the editors reported that censorship had occurred during the two and one-half years covered by the study.

At 82 per cent of the schools, the dean of students had occasion to discuss the advisability of a planned editorial with the editor. Of all deans only 2 per cent told the editor that the editorial could not be printed. Another 11 per cent asked the faculty adviser to persuade the editor not to print it. The largest group of deans, 38 per cent, "discussed with the editor his responsibilities, institutional objectives, or matters of taste." An only slightly smaller group of deans, 31 per cent, said they "informed the editor of anticipated difficulties arising from untimely editorials, and let him make his own decision." It is clear from these figures that most deans have come into contact with editors over controversial editorials, and that the deans generally see themselves as taking a persuasive rather than a coercive role.

The editors are not entirely intractable. About 41 per cent of them consulted the dean before printing controversial editorials and 46 per cent say they have "voluntarily refrained from printing [their] viewpoints on a 'controversial' issue in order to achieve or permit [their] institution to achieve some high purpose." This was most often the result of being informed in "backgrounding sessions" of anticipated difficulties resulting from untimely editorials, or of researching the situation on the editor's own initiative.

In spite of the censoring, consultation, and research which take place before publication, controversial editorials sometimes are published. We asked what disciplinary action, if any, followed. The deans consistently reported less disciplinary activity than did the student editors, but even according to the editors little action was taken in the two and one-half years covered by the study. They reported that the publication was suspended briefly at 3 per cent of all schools, the adviser was removed at 3 per cent, the publication was placed on probation at 2 per cent, money was withdrawn at 2 per cent, and the publication was banned at .6 per cent. Altogether, disciplinary action was taken at fewer than 11 per cent of the schools. Some person or group had urged the removal of the student editor from office for his position on controversial issues at 13 per cent of the schools according to the deans, and at 20 per cent of the schools according to the student editor, who is probably more sensitive to attacks on himself. The editor was actually removed at 5.6 per cent of all schools according to editors, and 3.6 per cent according to deans—this in a two-and-one-half-year period.

Severe disciplinary measures are thus sometimes, but infrequently, taken. We also asked how often the editor was censured for his publications. About half the editors reported that they had been privately censured and in one-fourth of the schools the censurer was a member of the administration. Fewer than one-fourth of all editors reported that they had been publicly censured but only 7 per cent said administrators did the censuring. Of all editors, 17 per cent were asked to retract statements, 16 per cent were asked to print apologies, and 24 per cent were asked not to express similar viewpoints in the future. Opposition on this scale does not seem unreasonable for editors who take stands on controversial issues, but subtle effects of censure may be great for subsequent editiorializing.

What is a controversial issue? Three-fourths of all editors said they had recently published editorials expressing their viewpoints on "controversial" issues, and we asked them to characterize the nature of these issues. The range of response was varied but in many cases the issues were local in nature. Here are a few examples given by editors themselves: "Stealing on campus—had been hushed up so as not to ruin 'image' of college"; "Should we have a Homecoming Queen?"; "What kind of music should we use at our church?"; "What kind of movies should be shown on campus?"; "Opposition to football scholarships." These issues are not the nationally divisive topics of social conflict with which we deal elsewhere in this study. Editorial freedom is, however, an important aspect of student freedom, and a newspaper should be free to discuss issues of immediate importance to its constituency, as well as to consider matters of importance and interest to society at large. It seems to us unnecessary that campus controversy should be restricted in many cases to local issues, and unreasonable that censorship should be employed even in these cases.

As Roger Ebert, a former president of the U.S. Student Press Association and editor of the *Daily Illini,* points out in a short, cogent essay on editorial freedom,[1] the institution is held legally accountable for any libel suits arising from the student newspaper's activities, so long as the institution is the publisher of the newspaper. Consequently, some form of censorship is only prudent. However, as Ebert also points out, there is no need for the university to be the publisher of the student paper. Many fine college newspapers are published by independent, financially sound student corporations. Such newspapers include, according to Ebert, the *Harvard Crimson, Michigan Daily, Cornell Daily Sun, Daily Texan, Daily Illini,* and *Rutgers Daily Targum.* Ebert points out that even for the many college newspapers that cannot finance themselves, accepting money from the college, thus making the college the legally responsible publisher, need not be the answer to the problem. He cites

[1] Roger Ebert, "Plain Talk on College Newspaper Freedom," *NASPA* (Journal of the Association of Deans and Administrators of Student Affairs), Vol. 2, No. 1 (July 1964), p. 9.

two other workable solutions. The first is to combine the yearbook and newspaper allowing the first to support the second financially. The second is to establish a nonprofit foundation attached to the university for the purpose of underwriting the operations of the student newspaper. Either of these solutions absolves the university from legal liability for the publication and allows it to disclaim any responsibility for the views expressed by the editor. It also forces the editor to assume directly the responsibility for his publication vis-à-vis the community, rather than having the administration as a buffer.

Where does censorship take place? Fifteen per cent of all editors had experienced censorship, contrary to their wishes, before publication. These editors were primarily at Catholic universities and liberal arts colleges, and at teachers' colleges. Thirty-three per cent of Catholic university editors, 30 per cent of Catholic liberal arts college editors, and 23 per cent of teachers' college editors had experienced such censorship. No such censorship had reportedly occurred at large public universities or at Protestant universities. Significantly less than average censorship took place at small public universities, private universities and liberal arts colleges, and Protestant liberal arts colleges. The data are presented in Table 21.

As for censuring editors following publication of controversial editorials, this was most marked at small public universities, Protestant liberal arts colleges, and, especially, at Catholic universities (see Table 21). It was found least often at Catholic liberal arts colleges. The removal of the editor had been urged most frequently at large and small public universities, and at private and Catholic universities, least frequently at technical institutions and Catholic liberal arts colleges. The editor had actually been removed least often at small public universities and at Catholic liberal arts colleges and removed most often at Catholic universities.

What does this pattern indicate? At Catholic liberal arts colleges there is considerable censorship before publication, little censuring after the fact, and the removal of the editor is seldom urged or accomplished. Censorship would seem to be highly effective at these colleges in preventing the expression of viewpoints unacceptable to the administration or faculty adviser. At Catholic universities on the other hand, prepublication censorship is prevalent but so is censuring, urging the removal of the editor, and actually removing him. Censorship seems ineffective

132

Table 21. Percentage of Student Editors, by Institutional Category, Responding Affirmatively to Questions about Censorship and Censure

	Universities					Colleges					All Categories
Question	Large Public	Small Public	Private	Protestant	Catholic	Private	Protestant	Catholic	Teachers'	Technical	
Has censorship occurred against your wishes during the past two and one-half years?	0**	10*	7**	0**	33**	11*	8**	30**	23**	17	15
During the past two and one-half years have you or your predecessor written editorials on controversial issues for which you were:											
Privately censured?	33**	51	58**	50	70**	47	50	50	43*	41	48
Publicly censured?	27*	27*	29*	23	37**	24	18*	11**	24	34**	22
Asked to retract?	16	17	22	27**	15	15	12**	15	19	24	17
Asked to print apology?	22*	17	24**	18	22*	15	18	8**	14	14	16
Asked not to express similar viewpoints in the future?	11*	29*	18*	27	33**	13**	28*	23	29*	21	24
Editors indicating some form of censure	62	70**	64	64	78**	65	72**	56**	66	66	66

* This percentage is significantly different from the percentage for all categories at the .05 level.
** This percentage is significantly different from the percentage for all categories at the .01 level.

133

in these universities and the editors report rebellious behavior. At large and small public and private universities censorship is uncommon and the removal of the editor is frequently urged but seldom accomplished. Conflict seems to be relatively common and acceptable without severely endangering the editor's tenure. At private liberal arts colleges and Protestant universities and colleges censorship is relatively uncommon, but only an average amount of conflict takes place. The editors are evidently more cautious, relative to their constituency. At technical institutions an average amount of censorship occurs but the removal of an editor is seldom urged. Evidently very little conflict takes place in these schools. Teachers' colleges report above average censorship, but only average censuring or urging of the editor's removal. These editors seem content to follow the censor's dictates.

It seems clear from these data that editorial freedom exists in some places, but that there is a common pattern of administrative review and control through the budget, censorship before the fact, and censuring or discipline after the fact. The student editor seems to work closely with the administration, and although the administration does not often exercise its control through overt disciplinary action this is probably because, working closely with the editor, it does not need to do so. The editor knows beforehand what is permitted and what is not.

Students in Policy-Making

In the thirteenth century the University of Bologna was administered entirely by students. It was required that the rector be a student and the compulsory retirement age was twenty-five. Times have changed. Today, students are typically without *direct* control over the quality or curriculum of the education they pay to receive, or the environment in which they receive it. But do they influence the making of policies about their education? If so, how clearly is the student voice heard in administrative circles? Are students "slaves of the system" or to some extent, at least, architects of their education?

In 61 per cent of the schools responding to our survey, according to deans, students hold membership in administrative policy-making committees and in almost 85 per cent of these schools this membership brings with it the right to vote. In order to appraise the efficacy of student participation in these committees, we asked the president and dean of students, "How relevant or helpful do you appraise the contributions of such student participation to be?" We also asked the student body president, "In your opinion, what, if any, benefits accrue to the university and students by their participation in policy-making?" Again, there was a wide range of response including agreement, qualification, and disagreement with the idea that participation is beneficial. A considerable number of benefits and disadvantages were identified by both students and administrators.

Students who felt their participation was useful to the university offered four reasons to explain this position:

First, student participation in policy-making enables the administration to "preview" student opinion, while students have an opportunity to change "unrealistic" administration-proposed policies. Second . . . the usually faulty communications between students and administration are improved: students are less likely to protest policy changes which are as much theirs as the administration's.

Basically, the only way to determine student needs . . . is to consult students.

[The student] point of view, though often lacking years of experience, can provide a fresh approach to college problems.

Some also mentioned benefits to the students:

The students learn the complexities which affect policy-making decisions. Actually, the arrangement makes sense when one considers that the administration wants to offer the environment for the best education. The student wants the best education available to him.

This "responsible freedom" allows opportunity for the full growth of the student.

Thus students argue that participation in policy-making improves administration-student communications channels, wins student support for new policies, assures that policies are aimed at the real needs of the students, provides a source of suggested new solutions to old problems, educates the students who participate, and helps ensure the best education for all the students.

College presidents were often enthusiastic in describing the benefits of this student participation:

They [students] often shed a different light on a given situation and assist the administration in gaining the proper perspective on problems of policy. It also serves as training in citizenship for the student representatives. . . . We have a good deal of respect for the serious thinking of our student leaders.

If anything, there is too little participation to please me. I believe a student body with some "pride of authorship" is more closely identified with the college.

[This is] highly important in order to make certain that students and staff are in touch with each other's points of view.

A few very small schools indicated that their special situations made formal participation unnecessary by students, and that the same ends were achieved informally:

Our school is small, is almost all Catholic, and is run primarily by Catholic priests. There is a very close relationship between faculty and students bordering on a family relationship. As a consequence, the matters referred to in this questionnaire are to a very large extent settled by daily person to person interplay and contact rather than by any written legislation.

These responses are from the large group of college presidents (77 per cent) who shared the students' belief that student participation was valuable both to the institution and to the student representatives and student body.

There was another group of schools where conflict seemed prevalent and administrators somewhat skeptical about the value of student participation. One student described his policy-making committee meetings by saying, "It's usually students vs. faculty, and so such activities sharpen our wits." This may serve an educational goal but it hardly seems an advisable method of running a productive committee. An irritant which may be partly responsible for this kind of discontent is the smug attitude of one college president who wrote, "By and large, we know what students will say in advance of any situation." However, certain presidents still seemed willing to tolerate student participation in policy-making although they were not quite sure why.

Not too helpful and not very relevant, but important to maintain and encourage.

We feel it could be helpful to all concerned. At least we sense it to .be the modern trend.

Another president recognized the benefits but then described one of the costs, saying it was "very time consuming as one is always breaking

136

in new student committee members." Other presidents emphasized the need for selectivity in accepting student comments but also said they were willing to listen.

[There is a] need to separate immature reaction and too agreeable comments from worthwhile statements.

Students look with an extremely biased eye. Their opinions are helpful but a good deal of it must be "sifted." Most students seek to justify their own whims—grind their own axes. However, I would not make a major policy decision directly related to students without getting their participation.

[It is] most helpful when it reflects reactions to their own college experience, involves their own responsible decisions, or reflects student attitudes; least helpful on the "larger" questions of policy and practice when neither knowledge nor experience can support judgment. But you can never tell when student opinion may prove interesting or suggestive.

These presidents suspected that student representatives might represent only their own personal opinions, that they might be flatterers, or that they would delay the work of the committee. Nonetheless, they were willing to hear student views because they knew there was wheat mixed with the chaff.

There was a third type of institution whose students responded with bitterness and complaints of neglect, and whose presidents reported that student advice was useless or worse. Here are excerpts from a few presidential comments:

Students are trying to become involved in school policies to too great an extent.

We have not had such participation, because we do not feel students have sufficient maturity to be policy makers. They may make suggestions at a lower level.

They have not experience enough and sometimes it prevents the committee work from progressing. The student population has to change too frequently.

Lack of experience, lack of expert knowledge, lack of time (and inclination) to explore thoroughly all the facts involved, all tend to render their advice ineffectual.

The students in these institutions were not enthusiastic in praising the benefits of their participation in policy-making committees. Asked about benefits one replied, "None, because it is such a façade." Another reported, "We have been explicitly told that we were 'not running the college.'" Administrators taking this approach apparently preferred legalistic accuracy to tact. One student thought the major benefit of committee meetings was "a lot of free lunches." Another asserted participation brought no advantages to the college "because the administration goes its own 'merry way.' Only if sufficient student pressure (from the campus at large) is exerted is there the possibility of changing policy." One student body president described what he was doing to win freedom from an administration he perceived to be intractable:

My university . . . is very, very conservative in philosophy. All the members of our Board of Trustees are well-to-do conservative businessmen or professional men. We have a history of iron-handed administration on contacts with the outer world. The result is that the student body looked toward social life rather than social controversy. It is only within the last three or four years that there has been any large scale awakening on campus. The student council is now emerging from a period of do-nothingism. However, the first step is to liberalize campus regulations. Thus, we have systematically attacked: 1. social rules 2. disciplinary rules 3. educational restrictions 4. speakers. We draft proposals and then try to persuade the administration to accept them. This is far from an easy task in an institution whose higher administrative officers (the vice-presidents (3) and president) very rarely see a student let alone ask his opinion. As long as the students are quiet and don't rock the boat the administration is satisfied. The student government has never been in serious trouble because it doesn't rock the boat—or hasn't up to this time.

It would seem, then, that the actual participation of students in policy-making, as well as the usefulness of this participation in shaping policy and in educating students, varies widely. As mentioned before, students do participate in policy-making committees in more than 60 per cent of all colleges. Furthermore, students have the opportunity to suggest policies or recommend changes of existing policies at 75 per cent of the remaining schools, according to both deans and student body presidents. This leaves fewer than 10 per cent of all schools where student opinions on policy matters are neither solicited nor volunteered.

The actual participation in changing policies is apparently somewhat less than the formal participation. In only about 40 per cent of all schools do representatives of student government or student organizations have the opportunity to review administrative policy changes before their adoption, according to both deans and student body presidents. In 50 per cent of the schools, according to the student body presidents, "individual students or representatives of student groups pressed for the change or clarification of some specific policy governing their expression on controversial societal issues" during the two and one-half years preceding the study. According to the deans, however, this had happened in only 30 per cent of the schools, so apparently a large proportion of the protest went unperceived by the administration. Change or clarification of policies actually occurred in 34 per cent of the schools, according to the student body presidents, so apparently student pressure was successful in two-thirds of the cases—a number about equal to the number of deans who perceived the pressure.

At what kinds of institutions are students most actively participating in policy-making? An analysis in terms of our ten categories of schools yields the results presented in Table 22.

At large and small public universities there is above average membership and voting membership in policy-making committees. The students have more often pressed for change or clarification of policies and the student government or other organizations can more often review administration policies before their adoption by the faculty and administration.

At private universities, according to the deans' reports, there is above average student participation and voting, and there is student review before administrative policy changes. The students, on the other hand, report only an average amount of such activity. Both students and deans agree that there is an unusual amount of student pressure for change or clarification. Perhaps at many of these institutions students consider that the committees on which they hold membership are not really policy-making committees but formal façades, and that the issues which are presented to them for prior approval are not major policy revision, but simply routine measures. The last effect is also observed at private liberal arts colleges.

At teachers' colleges and Protestant universities, students claim membership on administrative policy-making committees more often than administrators perceive this. At these institutions, perhaps, students are more readily impressed with the importance of any decision in which they are allowed to participate.

At Catholic liberal arts colleges there is below average student mem-

Table 22. Percentage of Schools, by Institutional Category, Responding Affirmatively to Questions about Student Participation in Policy-Making (According to Deans of Students and Student Body Presidents)

	Universities					Colleges					All Categories
Question	Large Public	Small Public	Private	Protestant	Catholic	Private	Protestant	Catholic	Teachers'	Technical	
Do students hold membership in administrative or faculty policy-making committees?											
Deans of students	91**	83**	71**	64	44**	72**	55**	32**	65	55	61
Student body presidents	82**	81**	62	77**	52**	66	66	38**	71**	66	64
Do students hold voting membership in administrative or faculty policy-making committees?											
Deans of students	89**	81**	62*	55	41**	62**	50	21**	57	52	54
Student body presidents	78**	73**	53	64*	33**	53	52	26**	64**	62	53
Have students pressed for changes or clarification of policies regarding student expression in the past two and one-half years?											
Deans of students	56**	46**	42**	36	19**	31	28	12**	33	28	30
Student body presidents	69**	60**	64**	55	63**	51	51	32**	48	41	50
Do student organizations or student government have opportunity to review policies governing student expression before adoption?											
Deans of students	58**	56**	51*	50	26**	40	43	30**	48	55*	44
Student body presidents	60**	41	36	45	22**	35	39	26**	41	55**	38

* This percentage is significantly different from the percentage for all categories at the .05 level.
** This percentage is significantly different from the percentage for all categories at the .01 level.

bership in policy-making committees, and below average voting on such committees. There is also below average student review of policy changes and student pressure for change or clarification of policies. At Catholic universities the same situation exists, with one exception: students, but not administrators, perceive above average student pressure for change or clarification of policies.

At 81 per cent of the responding schools there was a special committee for setting policy on student affairs. As indicated earlier, we directed a questionnaire to the chairman of that committee at the institutions where there was one, to ask him about his functions and the composition of his committee. Such committees are least common in the New England states and in the small universities. They are most common in private universities.

For about one-third of these committees the chairman is the dean of students. In most other cases the chairman is a faculty member, but on about 5 per cent of the committees a student is the chairman. At 75 per cent of the schools, the committee makes policies regarding the existence and functioning of student organizations. Other tasks for which some groups are responsible include the supervision of student publications and the setting of disciplinary policies.

Students have membership on 60 per cent of these committees and on 50 per cent they have full voting rights. In 44 per cent of these committees student members receive some orientation before participation in committee work. Although student participation is not universal, students who are not members of the committee may propose policy changes in 80 per cent of the cases. Major policy changes had resulted from student suggestions at 60 per cent of these schools during the two and one-half years before the study. Open hearings are sometimes held on policy changes at 46 per cent of the institutions, and proposed policy changes are sent to student organizations for review before committee action at about one-third of the schools.

Student voting participation is greatest at private universities (70 per cent) and at small public universities (65 per cent). It is least prevalent at the Catholic universities (19 per cent) and the Catholic liberal arts colleges (31 per cent).

Although this is only one form of student participation in policy-making, it is no doubt a highly strategic one at the 81 per cent of all institutions where such committees exist. Student membership on these committees opens new channels of communication, and provides students with the opportunity to convince administrative and faculty decision-makers that the scope of their freedom should be widened.

In conclusion, students participate in policy-making committees in a majority of schools and have the opportunity to suggest changes in many more. They have pressed for change or clarification of policy at about half the schools and have been successful in about one-third. Some formal channels of student participation in policy-making seem to be open at nearly all schools. Whether this participation is useful to students and/or administrators is a highly individual matter, and is probably the result of the design of the formal framework, the weight of tradition, and the prejudices and tact of both students and administrators. Where the participation works it seems to work to the immense satisfaction of all concerned, and where it fails the administrators' remarks are intolerant, and the students' comments are bitter and sarcastic.

The Student Body President

Of all students who might participate in policy-making or who might mediate between students and administrators when students desire more or different freedoms, the student body president is probably in the best tactical position. As the elected representative of the students, he is visible to the faculty and can speak with some authority. As one qualification for his job, he probably possesses some tact. Also, he is the head of an organization with a large constituency, and protected by tradition even when that tradition also includes inactivity.

It is unclear to whom the student body president is responsible or who is responsible to the president for supervising him. Of all student body presidents 67 per cent say they are responsible to the student government organization, 30 per cent to the dean, and 17 per cent to a faculty adviser—a number indicating multiple responsibility. According to the deans, however, only 44 per cent of the student body presidents are responsible to the student government, while 43 per cent answer to the dean, and 22 per cent to a faculty adviser. In view of the close working relationship between 95 per cent of the deans and student body presidents this wide divergence of opinion is remarkable. It would seem to indicate that suggestion and compromise rather than commands and obedience are common, so that the question of the formal

142

structure seldom arises. A similar disparity is found in analyzing information about who is responsible to the president for supervising the
student government. The student body presidents reported it was the
dean at 50 per cent of the schools and the faculty adviser at 31 per cent,
while the dean reported it was himself at 69 per cent, and the faculty
adviser at 20 per cent. These differences of perspective are much greater
than those found in considering the student editors' position. This is
probably because the student editor more frequently encounters conflict with the administration and in these situations the power structure
within which he operates is clarified.

The student body president almost never gets into trouble. In 94 per
cent of the schools no one had urged his removal during the two and
one-half years preceding the study, and he was actually removed at less
than 1 per cent of the institutions. The dean said he had taken no disciplinary action against the student government at 92 per cent of the
schools.

The dominant sources of funds for almost all student governments
were the college's operating budget and incidental fees collected from
students by the university. Less than 20 per cent of all college student
governments received more than half their revenue from dues (which
in many cases were compulsorily collected by the administration) or re-
ceipts from events sponsored by the student government.

Membership in a student organization represented by the student
government is compulsory at 76 per cent of all institutions, and at another 23 per cent there is a student government authorized to speak for
the students although membership in it by all students is not required.
In almost every case, the student body president is elected, not appointed.

In spite of the wide membership of these organizations, the student
body president did not often feel himself to be in contact with the majority of the students. We asked, "What percentage of the student body
shows enough interest in student government to make its opinions known
to the leaders of the student government organization?" The response
is depicted in Figure 17. Only 20 per cent of the student body presidents
reported that more than half of the students made their views known to
their leaders. Another 20 per cent indicated that they knew the opinions
of less than 10 per cent of their constituency.

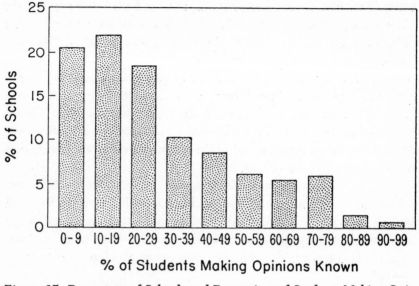

Figure 17. Percentage of Schools and Proportions of Students Making Opinions Known to Student Leaders (According to Student Body
Presidents)

What does the student government do? Student body presidents were
presented with a list of seventeen possible functions and asked to check
whether each was a major function, a minor function, or not covered by
their organization. Their responses to this question are indicated in Figure 18. It would appear from these responses that the major functions
of most student government organizations are relatively noncontro-
versial. The student government appears as an adjunct to the college
administration, relieving it of certain routine but onerous duties and acting as a mediator between administration and students. The most frequently perceived major function of student government was supervising campus elections—i.e., self-perpetuation. The second most frequently perceived was freshman orientation, an important and useful
task but hardly a controversial one. Third came organization of social
events. Participation in university policy-making on student activities
and the chartering and supervising of campus clubs were major functions at more than half the schools, and inviting speakers was a major
function at 38 per cent. Expressing student opinion and sponsoring
referenda on controversial societal issues were distinctly less important

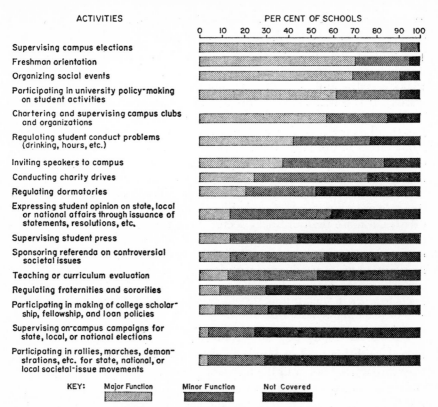

ACTIVITIES   PER CENT OF SCHOOLS

Supervising campus elections

Freshman orientation

Organizing social events

Participating in university policy-making
on student activities

Chartering and supervising campus clubs
and organizations

Regulating student conduct problems
(drinking, hours, etc.)

Inviting speakers to campus

Conducting charity drives

Regulating dormatories

Expressing student opinion on state, local
or national affairs through issuance of
statements, resolutions, etc.

Supervising student press

Sponsoring referenda on controversial
societal issues

Teaching or curriculum evaluation

Regulating fraternities and sororities

Participating in making of college scholarship, fellowship, and loan policies

Supervising on-campus campaigns for
state, local, or national elections

Participating in rallies, marches, demonstrations, etc. for state, national, or
local societal-issue movements

KEY: Major Function   Minor Function   Not Covered

Figure 18. Percentage of Student Body Presidents Specifying Various Activities To Be Functions of the Student Government Organization

functions. From this listing it would seem that the first purpose of student government is to orient students and supervise and sometimes discipline their social life. Although it is not uncommon for student organizations to participate in policy-making, to invite speakers, or to deal
with campus organizations, the lack of conflict between student body
presidents and administrators suggests that their role here is that of
mediator between administrators and more radical groups of students
who are actually taking extreme stands on controversial issues. Student
body presidents are typically not pressing for new academic freedoms.

An examination of the background and personality of the student
body president serves to illuminate his role further. Eliot Freidson's

145

essay "Four Types of Student Leader" provides such a portrait.[2] According to Freidson's research:

The student body president tends to come from a small town. His family's income tends to be the lowest of all student leaders—less than $5,000 yearly—and his father has not been occupationally mobile [upwards]. It is consistent with this that his major source of financial support at college tends to be his own earnings and scholarships . . . The fact that he participates in more than six campus activities may be testimony either to the social necessities imposed by aspiration to the office of student body president, or his inherent sociability and taste for joining.

The aspirations of the student body president are characteristically towards areas we think of as public service—occupations with modest salaries, a more than ordinary security of tenure, and the performance of duties that have a high idealistic value. He tends to major in education or theology. Consonant with the demands of his anticipated calling, he plans to go to graduate or professional school after completing his undergraduate studies. Looking to the future, he both prefers and expects to work in such public service occupations as the clergy and public school teaching or administration.

The student body president conforms to the stereotype of the mild liberal, with his modest family background, the necessity to work his way through school, and his taste for a career that generally implies a restrained but secure style of living with compensating possibilities for dedication to an ideal—whether teaching the young or serving God. Such a person, if described accurately by Freidson, seems to prefer to work within the established institutions of society to accomplish good, rather than choosing to press for revolutionary changes of the system. Thus, he is probably more in sympathy with the college administration than with dissatisfied students. Further, his plans for graduate school and his need for financial aid make him vulnerable to a college administration which grades his work and writes his recommendations for graduate school. In contrast with this, the more rebellious student editor comes from a more affluent family and does not plan to do graduate work. All these factors, then, may explain the relative docility of most student body presidents.

When the functions of the student government are analyzed by our

[2] Eliot Freidson, "Four Types of Student Leader," in *Student Government, Student Leaders, and the American College,* edited by Eliot Freidson (Philadelphia, Pa.: United States National Student Association, 1955), p. 53.

ten-way classification of institutions, certain variations and patterns of emphasis become apparent. The results of this analysis are presented in Table 23, which indicates whether more or fewer respondents than average from each type of school considered the function to be a major one for their organization.

A factor analysis of the seventeen student government functions yielded five factors which we use here as a convenient classification for purposes of discussion. *Social functions* include freshman orientation, organizing charity drives, and planning social events. *Social-regulatory functions* include the supervision of dormitories, fraternities, and student conduct. *Political-regulatory functions* are supervision of campus elections, campus organizations, the student press, and political campaigning on campus. *Participative functions* involve the student government with the administration in formulating policy for the college, and include participation in policy-making, in curriculum evaluation, in inviting speakers, and in determining loan and scholarship policies. *Expressive functions* consist of expressing student opinion, sponsorship of referenda, and participating in demonstrations.

In large and small public universities the participative and expressive functions were of significantly greater than average importance. At Protestant universities the participative function was more important, and at Catholic liberal arts colleges it was significantly less frequently considered a major function. At Protestant liberal arts colleges both the participative and expressive functions were less important, and in the private liberal arts colleges and technical institutions the expressive function was less important. Both of these functions are highly germane to this study—they involve the student government in decision-making by the administration and in sociopolitical activity by the students. It is at the smaller institutions that these are less frequently considered to be major functions of the student government.

The social and social-regulatory functions deal with important aspects of student life but not those which are the focus of this report. The social functions tended to be less important at the large public universities and more important at the Catholic and Protestant universities. The social-regulatory functions were less important at the teachers' colleges and Protestant universities, and more important at the private liberal arts colleges.

The regulation of political groups by the student government is not

147

Table 23. Percentage of Student Body Presidents, by Institutional Category, Reporting
Major Functions of the Student Government Organization

	Universities					Colleges					All Categories
Function	Large Public	Small Public	Private	Prot-estant	Cath-olic	Private	Prot-estant	Cath-olic	Teachers'	Tech-nical	
Participative functions											
Participation in making scholarship-loan policies	13**	13**	2**	9	4	7	4*	2**	13**	7	7
Teaching or curriculum evaluation	29**	13	27**	32**	22**	13	11	9**	5**	10	13
Inviting speakers to campuses	53**	48**	58**	68**	56**	25**	26**	29**	37	52**	38
Participation in policy-making on student activities	69*	68**	53*	59	52**	73**	63	46**	67*	66	62
Expressive functions											
Resolutions expressing student opinion	33**	13	27**	9	0**	14	7**	17	17	3**	15
Participation in demonstrations, rallies, etc.	9**	2	7*	0**	7*	4	3	2*	5	0*	4
Sponsoring referenda	16	11	22**	14	7*	16	12	13	15	14	14
Political-regulatory functions											
Supervising campus elections	82**	90	80**	100**	93	85**	96**	94	94	100**	92
Chartering campus clubs and organizations	67*	44	60	36**	74**	54*	46**	75**	63	66	59
Supervising student press	9*	21**	7**	27**	0**	19*	17*	7**	18*	10	14
Supervising political campaigning on campus	2	5	4	0*	0**	1**	5	5	7**	7	4
Social-regulatory functions											
Regulating dormitories	11**	14**	13**	14*	19	34**	22	30**	17	17	21
Regulating student conduct problems	42	46	36	23**	30**	55**	47*	44	34**	38	42
Regulating fraternities and/or sororities	9	10	13*	9	19**	9	6*	5**	10	10	9
Social functions											
Organizing social events	38**	60**	53**	82**	81**	67	72	79**	76**	66	69
Freshman orientation	49**	68	67	68	85**	71	74	71	74	79	71
Organizing charity drives	31	33**	22	50**	33*	26	23	22*	21	21	26

* This percentage is significantly different from the percentage for all categories at the .05 level.
** This percentage is significantly different from the percentage for all categories at the .01 level.

148

necessarily associated with freedom. Most student organizations would prefer not to be regulated at all, even by other students. On the other hand, they would probably prefer regulation by students to regulation by the administration. These regulatory activities were of more than average importance at teachers' colleges and less than average at private universities and liberal arts colleges.

Thus, at large and small public universities the emphasis of student government is especially on the issues treated in this study. The reverse is the case at Protestant liberal arts colleges. In the other types of schools the patterns of variation in the functions of the student government are complex and largely irrelevant to our purposes.

Many aspects of students' academic freedom and its determination have now been treated in detail. In the following chapter an over-all view will be taken to identify the general patterns of freedom and restraint in American educational institutions.

8 ✔

Where Is Freedom Enjoyed?

To WHAT extent are the currently controversial forms of academic freedom we have been discussing enjoyed by students? At which types of
higher educational institutions are each of these freedoms most or
least prevalent? The answers to such questions are complex. There are
variations among institutions in terms of the racial composition of the
student body, geographical location, size of enrollment, purpose of the
curriculum, and mission of the controlling authority. Indeed, freedom
itself is not a simple, unidimensional phenomenon. There is freedom of
discussion, freedom to invite speakers, freedom of organized protest,
freedom with regard to civil rights issues, and freedom for student newspaper editors, for student body presidents, and for students in policy-
making within the institutional framework. Furthermore, pressure for
change by students and the educational philosophy of administrators
in each institution must be separately considered. Finally, respondents
in the same institution do not always agree in their evaluations of the
freedom that students do enjoy. When administrators report one thing
and students another, which perception of reality, if either, is the more
accurate?

To simplify our answers to such problems, data have been presented
separately for each of the aspects of student academic freedom which
have been previously discussed. In this final chapter these findings will
be summarized briefly and then a number of different analyses will be

150

presented. Each of the ten types of schools will be separately discussed with reference to each type of academic freedom. In this way a comprehensive picture of each type of school will be delineated. Of course there are individual colleges within each type which do not conform to the general picture, but these are the exceptions. The ten categories adequately discriminate for the variables of size, type of curriculum, and controlling body. We will also discuss variations of student freedom in terms of geographical location of the institution and the race components of the student body. An additional section will summarize the findings concerning the agreement among our respondents. By presenting data in these ways previous findings can be summarized and new patterns of interpretation identified.

Climate, Philosophy, and Types of Freedom

Most administrators agreed with the proposition that "an *essential* part of the education of *each student* is the freedom to hear, critically examine, and *express viewpoints* on a *range* of positions held and advocated regarding issues that divide our society." In addition, most administrators reported that more students were becoming more openly demonstrative in expressing their views on controversial societal issues. Judging from their stated educational philosophy, one would expect most administrators to approve of this trend, yet our data show wide discrepancies between the administrators' philosophical commitment to student freedom and the actual freedom students report that they enjoy.

Among a list of student organizations whose purposes are political or social action, only the Young Democrats and Young Republicans were identified as functioning on approximately three-fourths of the nation's campuses. Of the other organizations, some were forbidden and most simply did not exist on any large number of campuses. It should be kept in mind that since many student organizations are local groups rather than nationally organized bodies there are probably student groups on many campuses which were not detected and reported by our respondents.

When asked whether student organizations advocating unpopular viewpoints could publicly express their positions on fourteen controversial issues, the great majority of administrators said "yes," and the student respondents generally agreed with them. If a student group

151

wished to invite an off-campus speaker, however, much depended on the type of institution and on the reputation of the speaker. Earl Warren could appear in 95 per cent of American colleges but George Lincoln Rockwell could be heard on fewer than one-fourth of the campuses. The range of permissiveness with regard to advocacy and action by student groups was almost as great. Only one-fourth of the administrators considered themselves to be quite permissive with regard to picketing, but almost three-fourths would be quite permissive with regard to a resolution passed by the student council after a referendum. Civil rights activity elicited the same range of response—from about 25 per cent of the administrators who would allow picketing to more than 80 per cent who would permit Rev. Martin Luther King to speak. Students do have freedom of speech but their freedom to act on their beliefs or to advocate solutions to society's problems is limited and dependent on the reputation of the person they wish to invite to speak from outside the college or on the type of action they would like to take about issues dividing the surrounding community. The freedom to act is widely subject to university control.

Moreover, student leaders are often not free agents. For instance, the student newspaper editor is typically responsible to a faculty adviser or dean and the budget of his newspaper often is supervised by the administration. In 42 per cent of the schools student editors must submit editorial copy to some college official before publication. Censorship does occur and censuring after publication is even more prevalent. Cries of "fire the editor" are frequent, it should be noted, but serious disciplinary action is not often taken. Likewise, the student body president works very closely with the dean, and the administration generally controls the finances of the student government. He seldom takes any controversial action and he is aware of the views of only a small percentage of his student constituency. To be sure, students have voting participation in policy-making committees in about two-thirds of American colleges, but their actual influence in these committees is reportedly limited.

Private Universities

Universities classified as not controlled by the public or a religious body were significantly more permissive with regard to the freedom of students to discuss controversial topics, to invite off-campus speakers, to demonstrate actively, and to exercise freedoms concerning the issue of civil rights. The student newspaper editor at these universities was exceptionally independent, the student body president played an unusually active role in social controversy, and a wide range of student organizations for action on social and political issues was found on the campuses. Students in these schools clearly practice freedom more widely than do students at most other American colleges.

Administrators of private universities were more enthusiastic in their support of the philosophical concept of academic freedom for students than were those in most other schools. Also, the student and administrative respondents were in closer agreement at private institutions than in others on the matters of acceptable speakers, student demonstrations, and discussion of topics. Student freedoms as identified by our questionnaires are rather thoroughly established in these schools and our respondents are agreed as to their prevalence.

Although student freedoms are thus firmly established, in many private universities administrators perceive a significant increase in student participation in discussion and action on controversial issues. Perhaps the possession of freedom contributes to its exercise, and many students are pressing into new areas of controversy. Since in most cases these students enjoy the freedoms identified in this report they may now be seeking to extend their freedoms into such areas as curriculum evaluation or liberalization of social rules. This hypothesis seems to be plausible since in private universities students participate in policy-making to a limited extent. Indeed, it is likely that these students' freedom in political and social action seems rather the outgrowth of an administration-led tradition rather than the result of student pressure. Such an interpretation is supported by the fact that the idea of extending academic freedom to students was first suggested by presidents in private universities: for example, Charles W. Eliot's 1907 Phi Beta Kappa address at Harvard. Thus, students in these schools seem to enjoy freedom through the action of liberal masters rather than by participating themselves in the making of policies which grant them liberty. On the other hand, the explanation for the change in the climate of student expression in these schools might simply be that the turn to societal issues after postwar apathy met with few administrative restrictions.

Private Liberal Arts Colleges

The findings for private liberal arts colleges are the same as those described for private universities, with one major exception. The increase in student expression on controversial issues was no greater than average in private liberal arts colleges, while it was much greater than average in private universities. It is possible that in these smaller colleges, less often located in a metropolis than are the universities, divisive social issues erupt less frequently. Although students in these colleges enjoy freedom comparable to that of the undergraduates in private universities, their schools may more closely approach the tradition of the "ivory tower," and they are less inclined to exercise their freedom or to controvert about freedoms. Furthermore, the graduate students who may serve as role models in universities are not present for emulation in liberal arts colleges. Undergraduates in universities may more readily adopt the goal of graduate students—societal application of knowledge—and may therefore be more inclined to implement their conclusions about remedies for social ills through overt protest action.

It is not surprising that the most extensive practice of freedom should be found in private institutions: these schools are the most independent from political control. The state legislature has no cause to be offended by these students' political activities. Nor is there any religious body which insists on inculcation of the dogmas, or on adherence of the young to the moral, social, and political views of their fathers. Many of these private institutions are fortunate enough to have large endowments which free them from complete dependence on the continuing financial support of alumni.

Large Public Universities

The large public universities were significantly more permissive than the average of our institutions with regard to student freedom to discuss topics, to invite speakers, to demonstrate, and to apply these freedoms to the cause of Negro civil rights. The student newspaper editor at the large public university was reportedly exceptionally independent, the student body president devoted his interest to controversial areas to an unusual extent, and a much greater than average number of student organizations were actively interested in political and social issues. Indeed, it is evident that the large public universities practiced student academic freedom just as extensively as did the private universities and liberal arts colleges.

There are three differences, however, between the large public universities and the private nonsectarian universities. Respondents from the public universities reported only an "average" increase in student interest in controversial issues, the administrators expressed only an "average" commitment to the principle of student freedom, but students participate in policy-making committees to a greater than average extent. In private universities the change in climate and the commitment to the philosophy of freedom are both greater than average, while student participation in policy-making is practiced only to an average extent. Furthermore, while respondents in private institutions displayed an unusual amount of agreement, in public institutions the respondents showed an exceptional amount of disagreement concerning two dimensions of student freedom—speakers and situations—and only an average amount of agreement on the other dimensions.

These differences suggest that at public universities attempts to establish student freedom have not yet been consummated. Students and administrators are not generally in agreement about the actual limits of freedom as it is practiced now and, furthermore, no unusually large number of administrators show enthusiasm for the principle of academic freedom for students. The frequent participation of students in policy-making in these institutions may reflect the fact that in public institutions students are working for their freedom from the inside, rather than simply enjoying freedom conferred by administrators.

Small Public Universities

In the smaller public universities (fewer than 8,600 students according to 1961–62 enrollment figures) the situation is markedly different from that in large public universities. The freedom of students to discuss topics, to invite speakers, to demonstrate on social issues, or to apply these freedoms to civil rights issues is not significantly above the average prevailing in all schools participating in our study. On the other hand, the student editor is unusually independent, the student body president carries on functions of exceptional controversiality, and students participate in policy-making more often than in most schools. Like the large public universities these institutions have no unusually large number of administrators who are committed to the philosophy of freedom, and only a reported average change in the climate of student expression is perceived. Furthermore, respondents displayed unusual disagreement regarding off-campus speakers and techniques of student expression and only average agreement on other matters.

Evidently, student academic freedom is neither practiced nor advocated to an unusual extent in the smaller public universities, but student leaders are exceptionally independent and active in policy-making.

Why should the large and smaller public universities differ so markedly? Several considerations apply to public institutions. First, they are dependent on the government financially. Second, as public institutions, their policies must not run contrary to civil law. Thus, administrators may often be reluctant to tolerate illegal demonstrative behavior even when it is carried on in good conscience. Third, the student as citizen stands in an unusual relationship to the university. He is a part of the constituency of the government from which the university derives its authority to govern him. Moreover, some public universities are required by law to admit all high school graduates who are state residents as students.

The dependency of the university on the government and the necessity to support the law, even when it may seem to be unnecessarily oppressive, act as restraints on university administrators who might prefer to grant considerable student freedom. On the other hand, the special citizen status of students in public institutions may serve to encourage expansion of their freedoms. Thus there are both restrictive and permissive forces operating on public universities generally, but these do not of themselves explain the greater restrictiveness of small public universities. We must look for other possible causes. Their small size and local, less prestigious nature may make them more susceptible than are large public universities to pressures exerted by conservative citizen or governmental groups. Also, large public universities are usually influential in a larger community—as research and cultural centers attracting business and industry to the region, thus contributing to its prosperity. Consequently, local government and citizen groups may be reluctant to damage the prestige and reputation of the institution, which allow it to draw growth to the area, by limiting the freedom of its students or administrators.

156

Protestant Universities and Liberal Arts Colleges

The universities and liberal arts colleges under Protestant control display as groups substantially the same characteristics. The responses from these groups to questions on climate, educational philosophy, freedom with regard to topics, speakers, demonstrations, and civil rights activities, student participation in policy-making, and functions of the student government organization were not substantially different from the responses from all schools as a group. There was reported, however, greater than average independence for the student newspaper editor in both types of institutions. An average amount of agreement among respondents existed except about the issue of off-campus speakers, in regard to which there was more disagreement than in other types of schools. Exceptional disagreement was found between deans and student presidents at Protestant schools concerning the prohibition of liberal student organizations.

The Protestant universities and liberal arts colleges, then, seem to be about at the average of all American schools with respect to the philosophy and practice of academic freedom for students, as we have defined it in this study. But to say they are "average" is only to say that they are, on the whole, less open than are private universities and liberal arts colleges and the large public universities, and that they are more open than Catholic institutions and teachers' colleges. Since the less open colleges will be discussed later we will limit discussion at this point to the question of why Protestant schools may be less open than are the public universities and private institutions.

We have classified as Protestant any college so listed in the *Directory of Higher Education, 1961–1962.* In turn, the basis for that listing is the fact that the school classified itself as Protestant. At some point in its history almost every privately supported nonsectarian school in America today would have been so classified. The private colleges were almost all founded by some Protestant religious group. As these colleges gained in stature, endowment, and liberalism they found themselves both financially and philosophically independent of the churches which had founded them. Compulsory chapel was dropped; curricular religious instruction was no longer required; the church's financial support diminished in importance, or disappeared; and board members were no longer, at least in an official capacity, churchmen. There are many colleges which are today still in a period of transition from church colleges

157

to private, nonsectarian institutions, and in some cases to classify them as one or the other is somewhat arbitrary.

Since many private colleges are the resultant of an evolutionary process of increasing independence and liberalization in initially Protestant institutions, it is reasonable to identify greater evidence of existing student freedoms, both in theory and in practice, in the private nonsectarian institutions.

As described earlier, the large public universities have also grown out of smaller public universities and thus display much the same characteristics of independence and openness in relation to the smaller universities, paralleling the private institutions' relation to the Protestant schools. It would seem that there is the same evolutionary development of increasing independence, prestige, liberalism, and academic freedom for students in both relationships. Yet, to posit these relationships is not to explain the differences which have been shown to exist. It would seem likely that the degree of freedom for students in Protestant schools, while probably related to size, homogeneity of students, and degree of financial independence from outside control, is most clearly determined by the fundamentally religious purposes of these institutions. These institutions no doubt consider a major part of their educational mission to be the training and development of scholars whose intellectual achievements are guided by a firm moral commitment to the Christian ethic. Thus, all behavior of students, whether as individuals or in organized groups, is considered to be the province of these educators, to be molded and shaped in the context of an overriding system of religious-ethical values. To attempt to achieve this goal requires a type of supervision and control which is, indeed, reflected in the results we have reported.

Technical Institutions

These schools, too, are essentially at the national institutional mean with respect to the practice of academic freedom. But technical school students are not perceived by our respondents to be evincing any increased interest in issues of social controversy, and the administrators in many of these schools disagree among themselves about whether freedom for students to address themselves to controversial social problems is essential to education. In no other type of school was this the case. Evidently the kinds of freedom we are discussing in this report seldom arise as issues in technical institutions, or the president and dean would

reach some sort of agreement regarding the school's policy. This interpretation is borne out by the fact that, although respondents agree fairly
often that most speakers would be permitted, the listed speakers had
seldom appeared on the campuses of technical institutions.

The issue of student academic freedom with regard to the divisive
social issues under consideration in this study is a dormant one in most
of these schools. It is not difficult to explain why this may be so. Students
and administrators alike pointed out that technical school students tend
to be "conservative" (indifferent?), seeking to achieve competence or
distinction in their highly complex fields, rather than interesting themselves in the broader problems of society, which are difficult to quantify
and appear impossible to solve.

Technical students are not necessarily apathetic. They are perceptive,
imaginative, and have logical, disciplined minds. Yet their tendency is
to apply their intellectual abilities to the important but limited problems of science and technology. We hold to one obiter dictum: that even
if they are successful in their demanding professions, it is society's loss
that their interest and competence in the social application of their expertise have not been developed.

Catholic Universities

In Catholic universities there was an "average" amount of freedom for
student groups to take controversial stands on socially divisive issues;
for these groups to demonstrate their views in certain active ways; and
for students to participate in civil rights activities. On the other hand,
student freedom to invite controversial off-campus speakers was significantly below the national mean, as was the independence of their student newspaper editors. Few student organizations concerned with
controversial political or social issues were found to be active on these
campuses. The administrators in these schools, and in other Catholic
institutions, showed the least commitment to the concept of academic
freedom, but they reported the greatest increase in student activity within the two and one-half years before the study.

Catholic universities place more restrictions on the practice of freedom and evidence less commitment to the philosophy of freedom than
do public, private, or Protestant institutions. On the other hand, the
interest of their students in controversial social issues is increasing more
rapidly, according to the administrators. Since these students exercise

159

only limited freedom now, it is likely that they are seeking liberties which many other institutions already permit their students. Two questions thus arise: why do Catholic universities permit less freedom of discussion to students, and why are their students now evincing a greater desire for more forms of freedom?

It was hypothesized that small public universities and Protestant schools may practice freedom less because they owe their financial support to, and are controlled by, outside groups. Also, their students tend to come from relatively homogeneous geographical or religious backgrounds, thus tending to make them more susceptible to the authority of that geographical or religious group. These factors would seem to be even more applicable to Catholic institutions and indeed Catholic schools restrict freedom much more than do other institutions. Catholic administrators are members of a more clearly defined religious hierarchy than are presidents of most Protestant schools. Private school administrators are usually at the top of a hierarchy, and public school presidents often themselves occupy power centers and are able to balance one community interest against another.

It is instructive to note the specific nature of the freedoms concerning which Catholic university students are restricted. For instance, they can discuss most topics, demonstrate, and work for civil rights. But they can seldom invite highly controversial speakers, nor do they participate extensively in policy-making. The student editor works under much supervision. These restrictions are concerned with communication to the students. Students are not forbidden to express or talk out their views, but the information on which these views are based is restricted by the administration through the student newspaper and limitations concerning outside speakers. Of course, there are many other avenues through which opinions are introduced to the students— the mass communications media, for example—but this consideration of the broadest range of opinions and advocacies does not usually take place in the university context. While there are distinctive patterns of responses from Catholic universities these are not easily explained in terms of an assumption of control by a hierarchical authority structure.

Why are students in Catholic universities now reportedly showing a greatly increased interest in controversial social issues? In part, they share the tendency of all American students to concern themselves once more with social issues. Possibly Catholic students, seeing other students acting on their beliefs, desire the freedom to do the same. Further, the present atmosphere in the Catholic community itself is conducive to this tendency: discussion of major social problems and liberalization of doctrine is in progress. The increasing concern of Catholic students with the important issues of their world seems to be a natural correlate of the atmosphere of ferment among many other students and among Catholics at large.

Catholic Liberal Arts Colleges

These institutions follow much the same pattern as Catholic universities, with one important exception. Where university students enjoy average freedom to express themselves, Catholic college students are significantly restricted in freedom of expression. Thus, student groups in Catholic liberal arts colleges have less than average freedom to take unpopular stands on controversial topics and to engage in demonstrative activities, although considerable freedom is granted to act in behalf of civil rights. Like students in the Catholic universities, Catholic college students are restricted in their freedom to invite speakers or to participate in policy-making; the student editor is not nearly as independent as are most student editors; and many Catholic college administrators do not support an unqualified statement of the principle of academic freedom as strongly as do other college administrators. Also like the situation in the Catholic universities, an unusual degree of recent student interest in controversial issues is observed.

The same general explanations which were advanced for the restrictiveness of Catholic universities and for the recent increase in student interest apply equally well to the liberal arts colleges. The greater restrictiveness of the colleges might also be explained by reasons parallel to those advanced for the greater restrictiveness of small public universities compared with large ones and of private liberal arts colleges compared with universities. That is, the Catholic universities are, in the context of Catholic higher education, prestigious centers of power. Their administrators are more venerated and hence enjoy more independence than college administrators. Further, it is necessary for the universities to compete with the public and private institutions for young, able Catholic students. In order to do this, and to maintain the prestige of the institution as a center of learning, it may be necessary to grant greater freedom to the students. Graduate students in the university set an ex-

161

ample of active application of scholarship to contemporary problems which influences the undergraduates. Finally, the university is more likely than a college to be located in a metropolis and its students are likely to be more diverse and sophisticated, jealously guarding encroachments on their freedoms.

It is reasonable, therefore, to expect that greater freedom will be found in Catholic universities than in Catholic liberal arts colleges. However, in both types of institution a great increase in student interest in divisive social issues has been observed and reported, and it seems likely that liberalization of these institutions is in store. Respondents in Catholic schools disagreed strongly in evaluating the existing freedom to discuss political, economic, and particularly religious topics. They agreed, however, to a greater than average degree concerning the freedom to invite speakers. It is not clear whether the freedom to hear outside, non-Catholic opinions is one which the students especially desire but it is clear that they and their administrators agree, in general, that they do not enjoy this freedom extensively.

Teachers' Colleges

Teachers' colleges are, for the most part, publicly financed and they enroll high proportions of women students. Many have ceased to consider themselves strictly teachers' colleges since they are beginning to offer a wide range of liberal arts courses. However, all of these schools equip their students to fill teaching positions in elementary or secondary education, and many still emphasize courses about classroom methods.

In these schools there is less than average freedom to discuss topics, to invite speakers, to demonstrate, or to engage in civil rights action. The student newspaper editor is unusually dependent on the administration, and there are fewer student organizations on the campus dealing with social and political issues. But student participation in policy-making is about average. An average increase was reported in student interest in controversial social issues and administrators proclaim commitment to the principle of academic freedom for students.

While in large public universities more freedom was practiced than preached, in teachers' colleges freedom seems to be more preached than practiced. Although teachers' colleges are almost all public institutions they differ in several respects from the universities. One point of difference is that they are smaller. The large public universities exhibited

162

the most freedom, small public universities exhibited average openness, and the teachers' colleges display the least openness. Since these organizations are smaller, less prestigious, and probably much less important to the economy of the surrounding region, one would expect them also to be more susceptible to influence from outside pressure groups. Moreover, pressure from outside groups would seem more likely. If citizens' groups are sometimes offended by the beliefs of individual students or student groups in universities or liberal arts colleges, they would be much more offended if radical opinions were held by teachers in training, about to be placed in a position to disseminate their views among the young.

Also, according to respondents from teachers' colleges, students there are more moderate than students in most other types of schools, and they tend to avoid controversial viewpoints or activities. Like students in technical institutions they have often made their vocational choice and are now applying themselves to attaining the knowledge that will permit them to practice it, rather than involving themselves in issues important to society at large but not perceived to be immediately and personally relevant to their own educational goals. Furthermore, a large majority of teachers' college students are women. In our society an active political role for women is still discouraged and protective restriction of females is considered more appropriate than for males. Since the role of schoolteacher is traditionally a feminine one and the women who fill it are respected, they are expected to be morally upright but disinterested in practical conflicts. They are not considered fighters for societal causes. In view of this cultural milieu it is not surprising to find the teachers' colleges restricting their students' activities. However, since these students will be teaching in elementary and secondary schools, and preparing pupils to fulfill a responsible and useful role in a democratic society, it seems appropriate, indeed imperative, that they should themselves have considerable interest in the issues which confront society. Our data suggest that opportunities to develop such interests are severely limited for students of these schools.

Geographical Differences

Institutions of higher education grouped by the six geographical accrediting regions of the United States are, with few exceptions, not sharply differentiated with respect to their practice of academic freedom. Schools in the middle Atlantic region are significantly more permissive than average with respect to all four general categories of freedom: topics, speakers, situations, and civil rights. The New England colleges and universities are more permissive only with regard to speakers and civil rights, and colleges in the southern region are less permissive with respect to only these two factors. The western geographical region, composed of schools in California and Hawaii, is more permissive than average with regard to speakers.

Variations with Race of Students

Institutions with predominantly Negro enrollment proved to have administrators with a more permissive educational philosophy. At the same time, the practices of these colleges were more restrictive than those of institutions having white students with the exception of freedom to discuss religious issues, to invite highly reputable speakers, and to engage in civil rights activity. Many Negro college administrators were closely and uncomfortably constrained by pressures from the surrounding community. Negro colleges in the South tended to permit student activity favoring civil rights, but to discourage the invitation of speakers opposed to the rapid expansion of Negro freedoms. Conversely, white southern institutions tended to welcome civil rights conservatives and to discourage student action in favor of Negro freedoms.

Differences among Respondents

For every college included in the report there were responses to the questionnaires from the president, the dean, the student body president, and the student newspaper editor. Each was familiar with his institution but each saw it from a different vantage point. Each had a different set of experiences, responsibilities, and personal and organizational goals. Thus, even when asked specific questions—whether a topic could be publicly discussed by a student group, whether a speaker could be invited or a demonstrative technique employed—the respondents of the same institution did not always answer in the same way, both because of these differences in perspective and because of gaps in the knowledge or experience of one or another of the respondents.

In response to most questions the amount of disagreement among respondents was very small. This seemed an indication that the questions were eliciting opinions about facts (i.e., prevailing policy) rather than simply opinions about the ideals, about which there would presumably be less agreement.

One would expect the greatest disagreement to come not between the president and dean, or between the student body president and the student editor, but between the students and the administration—traditional antagonists in the struggle for student academic freedom. Analysis of the responses of student and administrative respondents revealed that on almost every issue students reported less freedom to be enjoyed by students than did administrators. That is, students thought the administration would be permissive less often than the administration indicated. As we have repeatedly suggested, this could be due to a tendency among students to exaggerate the restrictions placed on them in an effort to gain support for their cause: fewer restrictions. On the other hand, it could be the result of different interpretations of the word "permissive" by students and administrators. Suppose, for example, that a student group wished to picket a public meeting and the dean advised the students that this action would arouse the opposition of parents and alumni of the school, bring pressure from the local community, and possibly result in imprisonment by the local civil authorities which would prevent their attendance and hamper their performance in college. Then the dean might say that the decision was theirs and he would not forbid the picketing. This dean might consider himself quite permissive, allowing the students to do as they saw fit even though this might involve him in difficulties. The students, on the other hand, could conceivably consider this dean to be highly restrictive. They might interpret his friendly warnings as thinly veiled threats. In view of the possibility of this sort of misunderstanding it is surprising, indeed, that the agreement among respondents about the permissiveness of the administration's policy is as great as was reported.

There were exceptions to the tendency of students to perceive less freedom than did administrators. Students perceived more freedom with respect to the right of student organizations to invite highly reputable speakers to the campus, the right of student government to pass resolutions on controversial issues, and the right of student groups to petition a government agency. As suggested earlier, these exceptions may have been due to students viewing nationally known speakers and their own student government leaders with more awe than did the administration, or to students mistakenly believing that the constitutional right to petition applies to collegiate as well as civil situations. Thus, students do not expect their administrators to question the desirability and advisability of nationally reputable men, to limit the freedom of action of student leaders, or to restrict the freedom to petition.

There was also a tendency for students to perceive more criticism of the college from the outside community, more criticism of themselves by the administration, and more pressure by themselves on the administration. Students would seem to be more sensitive to opposition than are administrators.

Data were also analyzed to determine which types of schools showed the greatest agreement and which the least. The respondents in the private institutions showed the greatest agreement with respect to topics, acceptable speakers, and situations. Evidence shows that these highly permissive schools have well-established traditions and well-understood policies with regard to these freedoms. The public institutions, including most teachers' colleges and technical institutions as well as the libertarian universities, show the least agreement with respect to acceptable speakers and controversial modes of student expression. The policies of these institutions seem to be less clearly formulated and more open to misunderstanding. This interpretation is bolstered by the fact that while private schools are above average in their commitment to the philosophy of freedom, public universities, the most open of all public institutions, are at the mean: evidently their practice of freedom is less strongly rooted.

Little agreement among respondents in the Protestant institutions is found with regard to controversial speakers; the Catholic schools show the most agreement on this issue. On the other hand, the Catholic schools show the least agreement on the discussion of political, economic, or religious issues. Perhaps all Catholic observers agree that controversial speakers are prohibited but the policies with regard to free discussion are matters of current disagreement and debate. Free speech may also be the current issue in teachers' colleges, where there is much disagreement on policies of discussing political, economic, and religious issues.

Agreement or disagreement among respondents is an important element in the description of the various freedoms students do enjoy. Presumably when there is high agreement among respondents in an institution the estimate of enjoyed freedoms is more reliable. Inferences can be made that congruity of perceptions has resulted from clearer com-

166

munication of purposes and goals in the institution, or perhaps the congruity is a result of deliberations about "rights" students may exercise in the school and the writing of school policies regarding them. We suggest at this time that the degree of congruity is associated with the procedures employed in a particular institution for handling disputes among students, faculty, and administrators, but further correlates of congruity and patterns of freedom and restrictions will emerge with additional research. Figure 19 illustrates a particular pattern of freedom, and agreement about that freedom, which seems to be characteristic of many of the more open nonsectarian universities and liberal arts colleges. This profile is based on the responses of the five persons answering the questionnaires in a large midwestern state university. The implications of the profile are not yet clear because the analysis of these data has only just begun. At this time the techniques used to score individual re-

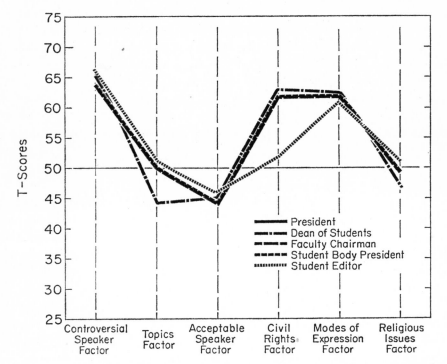

Figure 19. Institutional Profile Showing High Congruity of Perception of the Five Respondents from a Large Public University in the Midwest

spondents' questionnaires seem to require further refinement. Yet one thing is even now abundantly clear: there is almost perfect agreement among respondents in some schools and almost no agreement in others. To emphasize both the pattern and the congruity of response shown in Figure 19, we present as a contrast, in Figure 20, a most incongruous and seemingly patternless profile of responses from a small Protestant

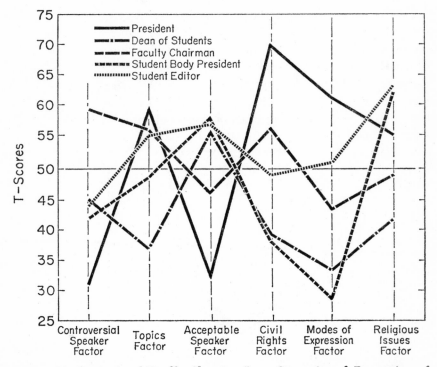

Figure 20. Institutional Profile Showing Low Congruity of Perception of the Five Respondents from a Small Protestant College in the South

liberal arts college in the southern region. We conclude that the freedom students enjoy in these two schools is quite different, but the nature and meaning of the differences must await further analysis.

Conclusion

Throughout this report we have attempted to view one aspect of a contemporary concern of higher educational institutions, to determine the forms and prevalence of student freedom of expression. By studying the phenomena through the methods of social science research, we have presented facts and some interpretations of those facts about the world of higher education. We have discussed the issues in an analytic framework which we hope will be productive of discussion. We have described and presented this world of fact in terms of simplified but useful categories.

Yet analysis begs the question of interpretation. How are the facts presented in this report to be made meaningful to the higher educational enterprise? The facts themselves tell us nothing about how they are to be used or interpreted. For example, an administrator who hopes to determine standards for his institution and to define the limits of student freedom at his institution by learning what freedoms now exist and where will be disappointed. He will not find massive support for his value system; rather, he will find some precedent for whatever decision he may choose to make, and regardless of the degree of freedom and the areas of freedom he wishes to establish for students, policies in some schools somewhere will follow his pattern, and he may conceivably consider them to "justify" his decisions. But an administrator seeking the consensus of his fellows will learn only that there is, today, little consensus. Diversity of practice among institutions is not surprising, since such determinants as the type of institutional control, defined mission of the institution, nature of the student body, the institution's governing body, influence of local community, and established precedent are overriding considerations. But the diversity in types of freedom granted within institutions is also extensive and may be surprisingly so in view of the fact that one might expect a university's policy to have internal consistency. Clearly a principle of absolute freedom for students does not shape university policy or such inconsistencies would not be so prevalent. It is rather the slow evolution of policy and established precedent that have determined, delineated, and limited or expanded student freedom. The overwhelming diversity revealed by our study is not surprising to most educators but it may be frightening to those who feel that diversity in the distribution of student freedoms is like diversity in the dispensation of justice.

However debatable may be the desirability of the diversity that has been revealed, the necessity for intensive clarification of the issues is undeniable. It is to be hoped that with greater clarification of issues will come further discussion of the values which underlie the practical question which John Stuart Mill so lucidly stated in his treatise *On Liberty*: ". . . the practical question, where to place the limits—how to make the fitting adjustment between individual independence and social control—is a subject on which nearly everything remains to be done."

APPENDIX

APPENDIX

The 1000 Colleges and Universities Surveyed

NOTE. The number 1 indicates no questionnaires were received from the institution. Of these 151 institutions, 26 did not respond to the invitation to participate in the study, 87 declined to participate, and 38 simply returned no questionnaires.

The number 2 indicates some, but not all, of the questionnaires were returned by August 10, 1964, when analysis of data was begun. Of the 154 institutions, 90 returned 4 questionnaires, 34 returned 3, 10 returned 2, and 20 returned 1.

The number 3 indicates the remainder of the questionnaires were returned following the analysis deadline.

ALABAMA
Alabama College
Auburn University (1)
Birmingham-Southern College (2)
Howard College
Huntingdon College (1)
Jacksonville State College (1)
Judson College
Livingston State College
Oakwood College
Saint Bernard College
Spring Hill College
Stillman College
Talladega College
Tuskegee Institute
University of Alabama

ALASKA
University of Alaska (2)

ARIZONA
Arizona State College
Arizona State University
University of Arizona

ARKANSAS
Agricultural, Mechanical, and Normal College
Arkansas Agricultural and Mechanical College
Arkansas College
Arkansas Polytechnic College (2)
Arkansas State College (1)
Arkansas State Teachers College (1)
College of the Ozarks
Harding College
Henderson State Teachers College
Hendrix College
Little Rock University

173

Ouachita Baptist College
Philander Smith College (1)
Southern State College
University of Arkansas (1)

CALIFORNIA

California State College at Hayward (2)
California Institute of Technology (1)
California State Polytechnic College
  Kellogg-Voorhis Campus
  San Luis Obispo Campus
California Western University (2)
Chapman College (2)
Chico State College (2,3)
Claremont Men's College (2)
College of the Holy Names
College of Notre Dame
Dominican College of San Rafael (2)
Fresno State College
Golden Gate College (1)
Harvey Mudd College
Humboldt State College
Immaculate Heart College
La Sierra College
La Verne College
Long Beach State College (2)
Los Angeles Pacific College (2)
Los Angeles State College of Applied
  Arts and Sciences (2)
Loyola University of Los Angeles
Marymont College
Mills College (1)
Mount Saint Mary's College
Northrop Institute of Technology (1)
Occidental College
Orange State College
Pacific Union College
Pasadena College
Pepperdine College (1)
Pomona College
Sacramento State College
Saint Mary's College of California
San Diego College for Women (1)
San Diego State College
San Fernando Valley State College
San Francisco College for Women (1)
San Francisco State College (2)
San Jose State College
Scripps College
Stanford University
University of California
  Berkeley Campus
  Davis Campus
  Los Angeles Campus

  Riverside Campus
  Santa Barbara Campus
University of the Pacific
University of Redlands
University of San Diego College for
  Men (2)
University of San Francisco
University of Santa Clara
University of Southern California (1)
Upland College
Westmont College
Whittier College (2)

COLORADO

Adams State College of Colorado
Colorado College
Colorado School of Mines (1)
Colorado State College
Colorado State University
Colorado Woman's College
Loretto Heights College
Regis College
University of Colorado (1)
University of Denver
Western State College of Colorado

CONNECTICUT

Albertus Magnus College (1)
Annhurst College
Central Connecticut State College (2)
Connecticut College
Danbury State College
Fairfield University
Saint Joseph College
Southern Connecticut State College
Trinity College (2)
University of Bridgeport
University of Connecticut
University of Hartford
Wesleyan University
Willimantic State College (2)
Yale University (2)

DELAWARE

Delaware State College
University of Delaware

DISTRICT OF COLUMBIA

American University, The
Catholic University of America
District of Columbia Teachers College
Dunbarton College of Holy Cross
George Washington University
Georgetown University

Howard University
Trinity College

FLORIDA
Barry College
Bethune-Cookman College
Florida Agricultural and Mechanical University (2)
Florida Normal and Industrial Memorial College
Florida Southern College
Florida State University
Rollins College
Stetson University
University of Florida
University of Miami
University of Tampa (2)

GEORGIA
Agnes Scott College (2)
Albany State College (1)
Berry College
Brenau College
Clark College
Emory University
Fort Valley State College (1)
Georgia Institute of Technology
Georgia Southern College
Georgia State College
La Grange College (1)
Mercer University
Morehouse College (2)
Morris Brown College (1)
Oglethorpe University
Paine College
Shorter College (1)
Spelman College (2)
Tift College (2)
University of Georgia
Valdosta State College (2)
Wesleyan College
Woman's College of Georgia, The

HAWAII
Chaminade College of Honolulu
Church College of Hawaii, The
University of Hawaii

IDAHO
College of Idaho, The
Idaho State College
University of Idaho (2)

ILLINOIS
Augustana College (2)

Aurora College
Barat College of the Sacred Heart
Blackburn College
Bradley University
Carthage College (moved to Kenosha, Wisconsin–1964)
Chicago Teachers College (1)
College of Saint Francis
Concordia Teachers College
De Paul University
Eastern Illinois University
Elmhurst College
George Williams College
Greenville College
Illinois College
Illinois Institute of Technology (2)
Illinois State University at Normal
Illinois Wesleyan University
Knox College
Lake Forest College
Loyola University
MacMurray College
Millikin University
Monmouth College
Mundelein College
National College of Education
North Central College
North Park College (1)
Northern Illinois University
Northwestern University (2)
Principia College
Quincy College
Rockford College
Roosevelt University (2)
Rosary College
Saint Procopius College
Saint Xavier College
Shimer College
Southern Illinois University
University of Chicago
University of Illinois
Western Illinois University
Wheaton College

INDIANA
Anderson College and Theological Seminary
Ball State University (2)
Butler University (1)
DePauw University
Earlham College
Evansville College
Frankin College of Indiana
Hanover College

175

Huntington College
Indiana Central College (1)
Indiana State College
Indiana University
Manchester College
Marian College
Purdue University
Rose Polytechnic Institute
Saint Francis College
Saint Joseph's College (2)
Saint Mary-of-the-Woods College
Saint Mary's College
Taylor University
University of Notre Dame
Valparaiso University
Wabash College

IOWA

Briar Cliff College
Buena Vista College
Central College
Clarke College
Coe College (1)
Cornell College
Drake University
Graceland College
Grinnell College
Iowa State University of Science and
    Technology (2)
Loras College (2)
Luther College
Marycrest College
Morningside College
Mount Mercy College
Parsons College (2)
Saint Ambrose College
Simpson College
State College of Iowa
State University of Iowa
University of Dubuque
Upper Iowa University (2)
Wartburg College
Westmar College
William Penn College

KANSAS

Baker University (2)
Bethany College (2)
Bethel College (2)
College of Emporia (1)
Fort Hays Kansas State College
Friends University
Kansas State College of Pittsburg (2)
Kansas State Teachers College

Kansas State University of Agriculture
    and Applied Science
Kansas Wesleyan University
McPherson College
Marymount College
Mount Saint Scholastica College (2)
Ottawa University
Saint Benedict's College
Saint Mary College
Southwestern College (1)
Sterling College
University of Kansas
Washburn University of Topeka
Wichita State University (2)

KENTUCKY

Asbury College (1)
Bellarmine College
Berea College
Brescia College
Catherine Spalding College
Centre College of Kentucky (2)
Eastern Kentucky State College (1)
Georgetown College
Kentucky State College
Kentucky Wesleyan College (1)
Morehead State College (2)
Murray State College (1)
Transylvania College
Union College
University of Kentucky (1)
University of Louisville
Ursuline College
Villa Madonna College
Western Kentucky State College (1)

LOUISIANA

Centenary College of Louisiana (1)
Dillard University (2)
Grambling College (2)
Louisiana College (2)
Louisiana Polytechnic Institute (1)
Louisiana State University
    Baton Rouge Campus (2)
    New Orleans Campus
Loyola University
McNeese State College
Northeastern Louisiana State College
Northwestern State College of
    Louisiana (1)
Saint Mary's Dominican College
Southeastern Louisiana College (1)
Southern University and Agricultural
    and Mechanical College (2)

COLLEGES AND UNIVERSITIES SURVEYED

Tulane University of Louisiana
University of Southwestern Louisiana
Xavier University of Louisiana (2)

MAINE
Bates College (2)
Bowdoin College
Colby College
Farmington State Teachers College
Gorham State Teachers College
Nasson College
University of Maine

MARYLAND
College of Notre Dame of Maryland
Columbia Union College (1)
Goucher College
Hood College (2)
Johns Hopkins University (1)
Loyola College
Morgan State College
Mount Saint Agnes College (1)
Mount Saint Mary's College (1)
Peabody Institute of Baltimore (1)
Saint John's College (1)
Saint Joseph College (1)
State Teachers Colleges
    Bowie
    Frostburg
    Salisbury
    Towson
University of Maryland
Washington College
Western Maryland College

MASSACHUSETTS
American International College
Amherst College
Anna Maria College for Women
Assumption College (2)
Atlantic Union College (2)
Boston College
Boston University
Brandeis University (2)
Clark University
College of the Holy Cross (2,3)
College of Our Lady of the Elms (1)
Emerson College
Emmanuel College (1)
Harvard University (2)
Lesley College (1)
Lowell Technological Institute
Massachusetts Institute of Technology
Merrimack College (2)

Mount Holyoke College (1)
Newton College of the Sacred Heart (1)
Northeastern University
Radcliffe College
Regis College for Women
Simmons College
Smith College
Springfield College
State Colleges
    Bridgewater (2)
    Fitchburg
    Framingham
    Lowell
    North Adams
    Salem (1)
    Westfield
    Worcester
Stonehill College
Suffolk University
Tufts University
University of Massachusetts
Wellesley College
Wheaton College (1)
Wheelock College
Williams College (2)
Worcester Polytechnic Institute

MICHIGAN
Adrian College
Albion College
Alma College
Aquinas College
Calvin College
Central Michigan University
Eastern Michigan University
Ferris State College
Hillsdale College (2)
Hope College
Kalamazoo College
Madonna College
Marygrove College (1)
Mercy College of Detroit
Michigan State University
Michigan Technological University
Nazareth College
Northern Michigan University
Olivet College
Siena Heights College
University of Detroit
University of Michigan
Wayne State University
Western Michigan University

MINNESOTA
Augsburg College

177

Bemidji State College
Bethel College
Carleton College
College of Saint Benedict
College of Saint Catherine
College of Saint Scholastica
College of Saint Teresa
College of Saint Thomas
Concordia College
Gustavus Adolphus College
Hamline University (2)
Macalester College
Mankato State College (2)
Moorhead State College (2)
Saint Cloud State College
Saint John's University
Saint Mary's College
Saint Olaf College
University of Minnesota
    Minneapolis Campus
    Duluth Campus
    Morris Campus
Winona State College

MISSISSIPPI

Belhaven College (1)
Blue Mountain College (1)
Delta State College (1)
Millsaps College
Mississippi College
Mississippi State College for Women
Mississippi State University (2)
Tougaloo Southern Christian College (2)
University of Mississippi
University of Southern Mississippi (1)
William Carey College

MISSOURI

Avila College
Cardinal Glennon College (2)
Central Methodist College (1)
Central Missouri State College (1)
Culver-Stockton College
Drury College (1)
Fontbonne College
Lincoln University (2)
Lindenwood College for Women
Maryville College of the Sacred Heart
Missouri Valley College
Northeast Missouri State Teachers
    College (1)
Northwest Missouri State College
Park College (1)
Rockhurst College

Saint Louis University
Southeast Missouri State College
Southwest Missouri State College
Tarkio College
University of Missouri
University of Missouri at Kansas City
Washington University (2)
Webster College
Westminster College
William Jewell College

MONTANA

Carroll College
College of Great Falls
Eastern Montana College of Education
Montana School of Mines (1)
Montana State College
Montana State University
Northern Montana College
Rocky Mountain College
Western Montana College of Education
    (1)

NEBRASKA

College of Saint Mary
Concordia Teachers College
Creighton University
Dana College
Doane College
Duchesne College of the Sacred Heart
Hastings College
Midland Lutheran College
Municipal University of Omaha (1)
Nebraska State Colleges
    Chadron
    Kearney
    Peru (1)
    Wayne (1)
Nebraska Wesleyan University
Union College
University of Nebraska

NEVADA

University of Nevada

NEW HAMPSHIRE

Dartmouth College
Keene State College
Mount Saint Mary College
Plymouth State College
Rivier College (1)
Saint Anselm's College
University of New Hampshire (2)

178

NEW JERSEY

Bloomfield College
Caldwell College for Women
College of Saint Elizabeth (1)
Drew University
Fairleigh Dickinson University
  Madison Campus
  Rutherford Campus
  Teaneck Campus
Georgian Court College (1)
Glassboro State College (2)
Jersey City State College (1)
Montclair State College
Newark College of Engineering
Newark State College
Paterson State College (1)
Princeton University
Rider College
Rutgers–The State University
Saint Peter's College
Seton Hall University (1)
Stevens Institute of Technology (1)
Trenton State College
Upsala College

NEW MEXICO

College of Saint Joseph on the Rio
  Grande (1)
Eastern New Mexico University
New Mexico Highlands University
New Mexico Institute of Mining and
  Technology
New Mexico State University
Western New Mexico University (2)
University of New Mexico

NEW YORK

Adelphi College (2)
Alfred University
Barnard College (2)
Bard College (2)
Canisius College
City University of New York
  Brooklyn College
  City College, Uptown
  City College, Downtown
  Hunter College
  Queens College
Clarkson College of Technology (2)
Colgate University
College of Mount Saint Vincent
College of New Rochelle (2)
College of Saint Rose
Columbia University

Cooper Union
Cornell University
D'Youville College
Elmira College (2)
Finch College (1)
Fordham University
Good Counsel College
Hamilton College
Hartwick College
Hobart College
Hofstra University
Houghton College (1)
Iona College
Ithaca College
Keuka College
Ladycliff College
Le Moyne College
Long Island University
  University Center
  C.W. Post College
Manhattan College
Manhattanville College of the
  Sacred Heart (1)
Mary Rogers College (1)
Marymount College
Marymount Manhattan College (1)
Mills College of Education (1)
Mount Saint Joseph Teachers College (1)
Nazareth College
New York University
  U Heights
  Washington Square
Niagara University (2)
Notre Dame College of Staten Island (1)
Pace College
Polytechnic Institute of Brooklyn
Pratt Institute (2)
Rensselaer Polytechnic Institute
Rochester Institute of Technology
Rosary Hill College
Russell Sage College
Saint Bernadine of Siena College
Saint Bonaventure University
Saint Francis College
Saint John Fisher College
Saint John's University (2)
Saint Joseph's College for Women
Saint Lawrence University (1)
Sarah Lawrence College
Skidmore College
State University of New York, State
  University Colleges
    Brockport
    Buffalo

179

Cortland
Fredonia
Geneseo (2)
New Paltz (1)
Oneonta (1)
Oswego (1)
Plattsburgh
Potsdam
State University Centers
  Albany (2)
  Buffalo
  Stony Brook
  Harpur College
Syracuse University (2)
Union College and University
University of Rochester (2)
Vassar College
Wagner College (1)
Wells College
William Smith College

NORTH CAROLINA

Agricultural and Technical College
  of North Carolina (2)
Appalachian State Teachers College
Atlantic Christian College
Belmont Abbey College
Bennett College (1)
Catawba College
Davidson College
Duke University
East Carolina College
Elizabeth City State College (2)
Elon College (1)
Fayetteville State College
Greensboro College (1)
Guilford College (1)
High Point College
Johnson C. Smith University
Lenoir Rhyne College
Livingstone College
Meredith College (1)
North Carolina College at Durham
Pembroke State College (2)
Pfeiffer College (2)
Queens College
Saint Andrews Presbyterian College
Saint Augustine's College
University of North Carolina
  Chapel Hill (2)
  Greensboro
  Raleigh
Wake Forest College

Western Carolina College (2)
Winston-Salem State College

NORTH DAKOTA

Jamestown College (2)
North Dakota State University
State Colleges
  Dickinson
  Mayville
  Minot
  Valley City
University of North Dakota

OHIO

Antioch College
Ashland College (2)
Baldwin-Wallace College
Bowling Green State University
Capital University
Case Institute of Technology
Central State College
College of Mount Saint Joseph on
  the Ohio
College of Saint Mary of the Springs
College of Steubenville, The (1)
College of Wooster (2)
Defiance College, The
Denison University
Fenn College
Heidelberg College
Hiram College
John Carroll University
Kent State University
Kenyon College
Lake Erie College
Marietta College
Mary Manse College
Miami University
Mount Union College (2)
Muskingum College
Notre Dame College
Oberlin College
Ohio Northern University (2)
Ohio State University
Ohio University
Ohio Wesleyan University
Otterbein College
Our Lady of Cincinnati College
Saint John College of Cleveland
University of Akron
University of Cincinnati
University of Dayton
University of Toledo
Ursuline College (1)

Western College for Women
Western Reserve University
Wilmington College
Wittenberg University
Xavier University
Youngstown University (1)

OKLAHOMA

Central State College
East Central State College (2)
Langston University (2)
Northeastern State College
Northwestern State College
Oklahoma Baptist University (2)
Oklahoma City University (2)
Oklahoma College for Women (2)
Oklahoma State University (2)
Panhandle Agricultural and Mechanical
    College (1)
Phillips University
Southeastern State College
Southwestern State College (2)
University of Oklahoma
University of Tulsa (1)

OREGON

Cascade College
Eastern Oregon College
George Fox College
Lewis and Clark College
Linfield College
Marylhurst College
Mount Angel College (1)
Oregon College of Education (2)
Oregon State University
Pacific University
Portland State College
Reed College
Southern Oregon College
University of Oregon
University of Portland
Willamette University (1)

PENNSYLVANIA

Albright College (2)
Allegheny College
Alliance College (1)
Beaver College
Bloomsburg State College (1)
Bryn Mawr College (1)
Bucknell University (1)
California State College
Carnegie Institute of Technology
Cedar Crest College (1)

Chatham College
Chestnut Hill College
Cheyney State College
Clarion State College
College Misericordia (1)
Dickinson College
Drexel Institute of Technology (2)
Duquesne University
East Stroudsburg State College
Eastern Baptist College (2)
Edinboro State College (2)
Elizabethtown College (2)
Franklin and Marshall College
Gannon College
Geneva College (2)
Gettysburg College
Grove City College (2)
Haverford College
Immaculata College
Indiana State College
Juniata College
King's College
Kutztown State College
Lafayette College (2)
La Salle College (1)
Lebanon Valley College
Lehigh University
Lincoln University
Lock Haven State College
Lycoming College
Mansfield State College
Marywood College
Mercyhurst College
Millersville State College
Mount Mercy College (2)
Muhlenberg College (2)
Pennsylvania Military College (2)
Pennsylvania State University (2)
Philadelphia College of Textiles and
    Science
Rosemont College
Saint Francis College (1)
Saint Joseph's College
Saint Vincent College
Seton Hill College
Shippensburg State College
Slippery Rock State College
Susquehanna University (2)
Swarthmore College
Temple University
Thiel College (1)
University of Pennsylvania
University of Pittsburgh
University of Scranton

181

Ursinus College
Villa Maria College
Villanova University
Washington and Jefferson College (1)
Waynesburg College
West Chester State College
Westminster College
Wilkes College (1)
Wilson College (1)

RHODE ISLAND

Barrington College (1)
Brown University
Pembroke College
Providence College
Rhode Island College
Rhode Island School of Design
Salve Regina College (1)
University of Rhode Island

SOUTH CAROLINA

Benedict College (2)
Claflin College (1)
Clemson University
Coker College
College of Charleston (1)
Columbia College (1)
Converse College (2)
Erskine College (2)
Furman University
Lander College
Limestone College (1)
Newberry College (2)
Presbyterian College (1)
South Carolina State College (2)
University of South Carolina (1)
Winthrop College (1)
Wofford College

SOUTH DAKOTA

Augustana College
Black Hills Teachers College
Dakota Wesleyan University
General Beadle State Teachers College
Huron College (2)
Mount Marty College
Northern State College
Sioux Falls College
South Dakota School of Mines and
    Technology
South Dakota State College of
    Agriculture and Mechanic Arts
Southern State Teachers College
University of South Dakota
Yankton College

TENNESSEE

Austin Peay State College
Belmont College (1)
Bethel College (2)
Carson-Newman College
Christian Brothers College (2)
David Lipscomb College (1)
East Tennessee State University
Fisk University (2)
George Peabody College for Teachers
King College (1)
Knoxville College
Lambuth College (1)
Lane College
LeMoyne College
Lincoln Memorial University
Maryville College (2)
Memphis State University
Middle Tennessee State College (1)
Milligan College
Siena College (1)
Southern Missionary College (2)
Southwestern at Memphis (1)
Tennessee Agricultural and Industrial
    State University
Tennessee Polytechnic Institute (2)
Tennessee Wesleyan College
Tusculum College
Union University (1)
University of Chattanooga
University of the South, The
University of Tennessee
Vanderbilt University (2)

TEXAS

Abilene Christian College
Austin College (1)
Baylor University (2)
East Texas State College
Hardin-Simmons University
Howard Payne College
Huston-Tillotson College
Incarnate Word College
Lamar State College of Technology
McMurry College
Mary Hardin-Baylor College (2)
Midwestern University
North Texas State University (1)
Our Lady of the Lake College
Prairie View Agricultural and
    Mechanical College (1)
Rice University (1)
Sacred Heart Dominican College
Saint Mary's University of San Antonio

Sam Houston State Teachers College
Southern Methodist University (2)
Southwest Texas State College
Southwestern University
Stephen F. Austin State College (2)
Sul Ross State College
Texas A & M University (2)
Texas Christian University
Texas College of Arts and Industries (2)
Texas Lutheran College
Texas Southern University (2)
Texas Technological College (1)
Texas Wesleyan College (2)
Texas Western College
Texas Woman's University (2)
Trinity University (1)
University of Houston
University of Saint Thomas
University of Texas (1)
West Texas State University
Wiley College (2)

UTAH

Brigham Young University
College of Southern Utah (1)
University of Utah
Utah State University of Agriculture
    and Applied Science (2)
Westminster College

VERMONT

Bennington College
Castleton State College (1)
Goddard College
Middlebury College (2)
Saint Michael's College
Trinity College (2)
University of Vermont and State
    Agricultural College

VIRGINIA

Bridgewater College
College of William and Mary
Emory and Henry College
Hampden-Sydney College
Hampton Institute
Hollins College
Longwood College
Lynchburg College
Madison College
Mary Baldwin College
Mary Washington College of the
    University of Virginia
Randolph-Macon College

Randolph-Macon Woman's College
Roanoke College
Saint Paul's College (1)
Sweet Briar College (1)
University of Richmond (1)
University of Virginia
Virginia Polytechnic Institute (2)
Virginia State College (2)
Virginia Union University
Washington and Lee University

WASHINGTON

Central Washington State College
Eastern Washington State College
Fort Wright College of the Holy Names
Gonzaga University
Pacific Lutheran University
Saint Martin's College (1)
Seattle Pacific College (2)
Seattle University (2,3)
University of Puget Sound
University of Washington
Walla Walla College
Washington State University
Western Washington State College
Whitman College
Whitworth College

WEST VIRGINIA

Alderson-Broaddus College (1)
Bethany College (2)
Bluefield State College (1)
Concord College (2)
Davis and Elkins College
Fairmont State College
Glenville State College
Marshall University
Morris Harvey College
Shepherd College
West Liberty State College
West Virginia Institute of Technology
West Virginia State College
West Virginia University
West Virginia Wesleyan College
Wheeling College

WISCONSIN

Alverno College (1)
Beloit College
Cardinal Stritch College (1)
Carroll College (2)
Carthage College (see Illinois)
Edgewood College of the Sacred Heart
Holy Family College

Lakeland College
Lawrence College
Marian College of Fond du
    Lac (1)
Marquette University
Milwaukee-Downer College
Mount Mary College
Northland College
Ripon College
Saint Norbert College (1)
Stout State College
University of Wisconsin
    Madison (2)
    Milwaukee

Viterbo College
Wisconsin State Colleges
    Eau Claire
    La Crosse
    Oshkosh (2)
    River Falls
    Stevens Point
    Superior
    Whitewater
Wisconsin State College and
    Institute of Technology (1)

WYOMING
University of Wyoming (2)

INDEX

Index

Date Due
